New Nordic Houses

Dominic Bradbury

with over 350 illustrations

Introduction

The houses of the Nordic countries are lifted by their intrinsic sense of warmth. Set within a climate that can be cold and challenging, as well as bracing and beautiful, the idea of a warm, welcoming home assumes particular power and resonance. Many different elements combine to create this unique and engaging Scandinavian character, in which the importance of the hearth plays an ongoing and crucial role. It is rare to find a Nordic residential building, whether traditional or contemporary, where the fireplace does not play a pivotal part, creating a focal point for everyday living and placing the idea of warmth at the heart of the home.

The factors that contribute to the notion of Nordic warmth are essentially the same as those that define the unique character of the region's architecture. Materials play a crucial part, with many architects continuing a preoccupation with those that are natural and organic, and lend texture and personality to a space. To think of Norway, Denmark, Finland and Sweden is to conjure an image, above all, of the wooden cabin or farmhouse, vernacular reference points that continue to inspire today's Nordic architects, who use timber as a 'modern' material, as they experiment with form, volume and space. Stone and brick, too, reinforce a palette that is rooted in the landscape.

The multiple threads of Nordic architecture lead back naturally and inevitably to this extraordinary landscape. The epic coastline, with its countless fjords, inlets and isles, contrasts vividly with the mountains and lakes of these glacial countries on the edge of the Arctic circle. Yet this is also a place of forests and woodlands, prairies and pastures, which inform the mythology and narratives of Scandinavia. Nature plays a profound part in shaping the art and culture of the region, and its architects exhibit a vital respect for the natural world. This is expressed in the choice of eco-friendly materials and a general emphasis upon sustainability, with the creation of houses that are super-insulated to preserve energy and often warmed by green sources, from solar panels to ground-source (or geothermal) heat pumps. A number of the houses in this book are off-grid, with architects and designers aiming for buildings that are fully self-sufficient.

This respect extends to the land itself, with Nordic architects taking particular care to make as light an impact on their sites and settings as possible. The ambition to touch the earth lightly leads to innovative structural solutions, such as raising homes above ground level on slim, supporting pillars to reduce the impact of the building, while landscaping is also kept to a minimum. There is the commonly expressed idea that such houses are temporary guests upon the land, and that they should be capable of being replaced or even removed altogether with little or no trace of their existence.

This outlook is linked to the over-arching respect for the natural world seen across the Scandinavian countries, and the accepted wisdom that the countryside and coastline belong to everyone. Countries such as Sweden have the right to roam (known as *allemansrätt*) written into their constitutions, and planning conditions across the region seek to limit the impact of new buildings by restricting height, scale and overall visibility. Many architects see such conditions as sensible challenges, rather than as limitations on their own creativity. The particular context of a project is an essential point of inspiration for Nordic architects, and, while this may include research into cultural, historical and vernacular points of reference, the most vital contextual element will always be the landscape.

'Our objective is to create relevant architecture that has its starting point in the specific conditions of the project,' says architect Bolle Tham of Tham & Videgård (pp. 72, 156). 'One factor that makes

House for a Drummer, Sweden,
Bornstein Lyckefors Architects

buildings so interesting and inspiring to design is context. When looking at a project's context, we find an inexhaustible source of inspiration for new solutions. One can argue that it is primarily this approach that determines if a project will work or not, both in terms of its location and its time.'

The importance of the physical and topographical context of the new Nordic house lends itself to a highly site-specific solution, in which the building is partially shaped by its surroundings. The composition of the structure sits in tune with the topography, but more importantly, it seeks a considered and thoughtful connection with the natural setting. Windows, openings and apertures frame key views, and there is a careful dissolution of solid boundaries between indoors and out, as living spaces within flow freely to terraces, decks, courtyards and verandas. The emphasis upon framing vistas on the one hand and eroding borders between interiors and exteriors on the other are essential characteristics of the Nordic dwelling and add to the overall sense of warmth, with nature playing a key role in the whole experience of being at home.

'There is something pragmatic in Scandinavian architecture that can provide an answer to any number of circumstances,' Norwegian architect Jon Danielsen Aarhus (p. 20) explains. 'Most importantly, there is a responsiveness to the landscape that is inherently unique and down to earth.'

Respect for context and the formulation of site-specific designs were also important considerations for Scandinavia's pioneering architects, who helped invent a version of 'warm modernism' in the middle years of the 20th century. Unlike other architects of the same period, who were devoted to the International Style – which was more concerned with universal, rather than specific, solutions to structure, circulation and form – the great Nordic masters advocated a greater sensitive response to settings and circumstances. This sensitivity was combined with an experimental and forward-thinking approach to modern living, breaking down the more formal floorplans seen in traditional and neoclassical houses and embracing such concepts as open-plan living spaces.

Alvar Aalto was one of the greatest proponents of this softer version of modernism. Structurally and spatially, his houses and buildings were fresh and innovative, but context was also a vital consideration. Typically, he involved himself in all aspects of the design, within a cohesive and fully rounded approach. One of Aalto's masterpieces, Villa Mairea (1939), in Noormarkuu, Finland, is surrounded by woodland. The interiors feature a central fireplace and an extensive use of brick and timber, while the timber poles supporting the staircase and raffia-wrapped structural pillars echo the countless tree trunks glimpsed through the windows. Here, and across many of the architect's other projects, the spaces are both inherently modern and highly crafted.

Scandinavia's strong artisanal tradition was a powerful resource and source of inspiration for many mid-century Nordic architects and designers. Other designs by Aalto, including the Korpikoto Hunting Lodge (1945) at Pertunmaa, or Villa Kihlman (1948) in Ylöjärvi and Villa Manner (1952) in Sondby, both essentially reinterpretations of the timber cabin, drew upon this craft tradition. While he continued to forge fresh ideas in projects such as his own Muuratsalo Experimental House (1953), the lessons and examples of the past stayed in his thoughts, and, rather than breaking with the past like some of his contemporaries overseas, Aalto continued to recognize the value of his own architectural and design history.

The Norwegian architect Wenche Selmer was also highly influenced by traditional typologies, combining timber and expanses of glass in her own house near Oslo (1963). Other modernist pioneers, including the Swedish designer Bruno Mathsson, sought to reinvent the Scandinavian villa, while employing a more open portfolio of materials and structural techniques in, for example, the Kungsör House (1954) and the Weekend Cottage (1960) at Frösakull. Yet his houses still possess a quintessentially Scandinavian sensibility, with their emphasis on context and indoor–outdoor spaces, including the veranda, which appears again and again in his designs. This open-minded process of nurturing both contemporary design and traditional ways of making continues to enrich Nordic architecture today.

clockwise, from left Gotland Summerhouse, Sweden, Enflo Arkitekter & DEVE Architects; Store Lauvøya-Bestemorstua, Norway, Mikado Arkitektur; Cabin Vindheim, Norway, Vardehaugen

Introduction

clockwise, from left Four Cornered Villa, Finland, Avanto Architects; Lille Arøya, Norway, Lund Hagem Architects; Manshausen Island Resort, Norway, Stinessen Arkitektur

10

In Denmark, Arne Jacobsen explored a wide range of structural, geometric and formal solutions as he sought to re-examine and remodel the country villa, from the Round House (1957) in Odden Havn to the rectangular precision of Upton-Hansen House (1954) in Kalundborg. He was also open to a wide range of material choices, including brick, timber and rendered façades. Yet many of Jacobsen's designs are defined by a degree of relative modesty, as well as a contextual approach, and infused with a warmth derived from materials, texture and colour. Siesby House (1959), a linear timber-and-glass cabin in Sorgenfri, appears to float above a modest basement level, faced in brick and tucked into the hillside setting. In this elevated position, the views

of the landscape from within this modestly scaled home are maximized to full advantage. Comfort is also paramount, with bespoke fitted furniture, storage and other integrated elements throughout.

This combination of modesty and informality was a common characteristic of the 'soft' Nordic modernism. Such homes were seldom large in scale or full of showmanship. Modern country houses were often single-storey and set low in the landscape, featuring integrated elements from galley kitchens to bunkrooms or small bedrooms reminiscent of a ship's cabin. This was true of Danish architect Halldor Gunnløgsson's own home overlooking the Øresund strait, which consciously combined Japanese and Scandinavian influences within a host of space-saving features and fitted elements. A Japanese influence can also be detected in Vilhelm Wohlert's Bohr House (1957) in Tisvilde, on the north coast of Zealand, a modern cabin featuring a run of hinged shutters on the façade, which creates a series of canopies that, when open, turn the terrace into a partially protected veranda.

A similar spirit of ingenuity suffused Erik Christian Sørensen's own home (1955) in Gentofte, also on Zealand, another single-storey, wooden home with an organic character, a crafted quality, a strong indoor–outdoor relationship and a modular framework, combined with lightweight and partial screen-like partitions that some connected with Japan, although Sørensen himself declared that he found all the inspiration he needed in the Nordic vernacular, particularly among its rural cottages and farmsteads.

The work of the Nordic masters and the notion of soft modernism continues to underpin residential architecture in the 21st century. So many of the qualities mentioned above – ingenuity, modesty, informality, connectivity, context – continue to define the enduring character of the new Nordic home. The original guidelines established by the pioneering modernists of the region form a kind of foundation upon which contemporary Scandinavian architecture has grown and flourished. Even as the value of context and tradition has been somewhat neglected in certain parts of the world, they have become even more relevant in Scandinavia, together with a renewed focus on sustainability.

Advances in engineering, construction and technology are put to best use to create a new generation of 21st-century homes that sit lightly upon the land, seeking to connect with nature with minimal impact on the natural world. Given its demanding and sometimes extreme climate, Scandinavia is at the forefront of energy conservation, with its highly insulated envelopes and triple-glazing, but also ahead of the pack in terms of off-grid living and renewable energy generated at source. Sensitivities about sustainability and environmental context are embedded in contemporary Nordic architecture, but without any compromise in imagination and invention. The houses featured in this book are full of fresh ideas and original thinking, with a dynamic approach to space, volume and form, and defined by their surroundings. They are also places of comfort and delight, with fireplaces, saunas, window seats and verandas. There is an essential warmth to the character of the new Nordic house that is hard to resist.

Rural Cabins

The ideal of the country cabin has particular resonance across the Nordic countries. Defined by simplicity and modesty, these cabins possess a lightness of touch that sits well within the natural beauty of the landscape. Largely made of timber and usually single-storey, they sit low in the land and have an organic quality that ties them to the countryside with subtlety and grace. In recent years, Nordic architects have increasingly embraced and explored the typology of the cabin as a way of creating a new generation of rural homes that possess an innate sensitivity to their natural surroundings. This 21st-century version serves as a kind of belvedere, or viewing platform, connected to landscapes that demand reverence and inspire delight.

The modern Scandinavian cabin has its roots in a number of traditional buildings common to the region. They owe much to the simple forms of timber barns and agricultural sheds, including the hillside and mountain huts used by farmers and shepherds. Other kinds of rugged mountain shelters used by hikers and skiers also inform the make-up of the contemporary cabin – including the Norwegian *gapahuk*, a basic roofed hut with one side left open, used to protect oneself from the elements. The endless coastline of the Nordic countries, with its archipelagos and islands, also offers another kind of cabin, sharing that sense of organic simplicity with traditional fishermen's huts and boathouses. Once again, it is the lightness of the materials and the availability of timber that help to make wood a natural choice in every respect, along with the crossover in craftsmanship between boat-making and house-building.

The strength of the Nordic craft tradition adds to the desirability of the contemporary cabin. Beautifully detailed exteriors are complemented by crafted interiors that feature much in the way of bespoke and fitted timber furniture, including seating and bunk beds, as well as kitchen cabinets and wardrobes. Materials are reduced to a modest palette of choices and finishes, reinforcing the sense of simplicity and cohesion. Contemporary architects possess a particular respect for these traditions and ways of making. 'What seems to be a common trait among traditional cabins is their simplicity in form, size and comfort,' explains Jon Danielsen Aarhus, who designed Cabin Ustaoset (p. 20), among others.

'So when modern cabins become ever larger, built in a romantic, ornamental style, with indoor plumbing and a driveway and a garage, they move away from the traditional building. The style looks misplaced, and the infrastructure destroys the very thing you want to get close to – nature.'

Yet the essential modesty of the cabin – reinforced in many parts of Scandinavia by local planning restrictions in terms of scale and footprint – does not mean that architects are limited when it comes to an imaginative response to context and setting. As the buildings in this chapter suggest, the contemporary Nordic cabin is rich in variety and depth, with a range of fluid forms, rounded interiors and a vivid sense of connection between inside and out, even within extreme and challenging settings. Snøhetta's cabin (p. 60) in the mountains of Hordaland, Norway, is little more than a single room covered by a sinuous roof, yet manages to combine many different themes and ideas in a small shelter with a powerful escapist allure. In Finland, Studio Puisto elevated their modern cabins on stilts, creating a series of original treehouses (p. 66), while Swedish practice Waldemarson Berglund embraced the gradient of the mountain of Åre in their design for a triptych of cabins (p. 84), which literally step down the slope.

In all of these projects, there is a particular emphasis on establishing a thoughtful relationship between building and landscape, linking interior and exterior space. Whether in a forest, island or mountain setting, terraces, verandas and decks have become integral parts of the design, with apertures and openings becoming lenses focused on framed panoramas. In this respect, today's architects owe much to the example of their pioneering modernist predecessors, as well as to traditional buildings. In the 1950s, Halldor Gunnløgsson built a home for himself and his wife on the coast at Rungsted, near Copenhagen, which could be described as a modern cabin: a single-storey home facing the ocean, with a semi-open-plan layout and indoor–outdoor spaces. Its crafted quality and extensive use of joinery had both Japanese and Danish influences. Similarly, the country house designed a decade later by Bruno Mathsson near Värnamo, Sweden, spliced modesty and craft with a fluid layout and extensive glazing that drew the bucolic landscape deep into the heart of the house.

The 21st-century Nordic cabins featured here draw upon such influences, as well as the craft tradition and the concept of organic architecture, in buildings that forge a deep interaction with their surroundings and embrace fluid floorplans that blur the boundaries between indoors and out. They meet a growing need for solace, escapism and a deeper relationship with nature as an antidote to the growing pressures of the urban, digital world.

Rural Cabins

Norderhov Cabin

Hønefoss, Norway

Atelier Oslo

The contemporary Nordic cabin takes inspiration from vernacular influences, yet updates and reinterprets them in fresh and innovative ways. This is very much the case with Atelier Oslo's Norderhov Cabin, an off-the-grid retreat that subtly subverts and reinvents the notion of the traditional dwelling. Outside, the form appears sculptural, with the house arranged as an irregular cross, and cladding made from slim basalt stone shingles instead of timber. Within, the interiors are fluid and open, rather than compartmentalized, maximizing the flow of light and allowing the entire cabin to engage directly with framed views of the surrounding landscape via substantial glass apertures that face key vistas.

The single-storey cabin is located on a forested hillside overlooking Lake Steinsfjorden, around 80 km (50 miles) northwest of Oslo. The town of Hønefoss, once home to one of Norway's largest paper mills, is not far away. The clients owned an existing cabin on the site, and asked the architects to design a modestly sized replacement. A key requirement – and challenge – was to make the most of the views of the lake and the forest, establishing a direct sense of engagement with nature. Stepping away from traditional rectilinear layouts, they created a design that echoed the shifting topography with an irregular cruciform plan, providing floor-to-ceiling windows and a small, sheltered veranda, tucked into the outline of the façade.

Many of the structural elements were prefabricated and brought onto site for assembly. The framework itself is made from laminated timber with a substructure of Kerto plywood, while the building is anchored to the bedrock with steel rods and covered by durable stone shingles. Used for both exterior walls and the roof, these shingles lend the cabin a sculpted unity, rather like a work of land art. The highly crafted interiors revolve around a central fireplace that forms a vital focal point, while sinuous plywood ceilings and joinery provide a soft, warm contrast to the cabin's stone skin. Rather than using solid partitions, 'rooms' are defined by the irregular shape and use of shifting floor levels, linked by a series of rounded steps that appear to morph into integrated benches and seating within a highly cohesive and fluid free-form approach. The key living spaces are open plan, arranged around the fireplace and the views, while the bedroom and bathroom are tucked away within the spurs towards the rear of the cabin.

The house is fully off-grid, with two solar panels providing electricity for lighting and a central fireplace for warmth. It also has its own water supply and waste-water system, and even the plywood comes from sustainable sources. 'The cabin has a functional yet comfortable character,' explains architect Juan Ruiz. 'There are no superfluous elements, as each one is necessary for the needs and wellbeing of the clients. What pleases us most is the integration of the cabin into the existing landscape, and the extension of this landscape into the interior spaces.'

Rural Cabins   Norderhov Cabin

The layout of the cabin is fluid and largely open plan, with the various zones defined by the shape of the building and the arrangement of fitted furniture and joinery.

Rural Cabins

Norderhov Cabin

Rural Cabins   Norderhov Cabin

Cabin Ustaoset

Ustaoset, Norway

Jon Danielsen Aarhus

The countryside around the Norwegian village of Ustaoset is famous for its picturesque mountain cabins, which feature in Jo Nesbø's crime novel, *The Leopard*, while the village itself forms the finish line for the Skarverennet, a cross-country ski race. Sitting upon the railway line from Oslo in the east to Bergen in the west, Ustaoset first became popular as a destination in the early 20th century, with visitors drawn by the powerful and rugged mountain landscape.

Today, building in the region, which contains a number of national parks, is strictly controlled. Architect Jon Danielsen Aarhus is fortunate to belong to a family that has owned a mesmerizing mountain site here since the 1960s that already had a small cabin. The location is relatively high in the landscape, at the foot of the Hardangervidda mountain, in an area with no road access and a natural environment that is well preserved and protected. From here, the views stretch out for 40 km (25 miles) and include the lake of Ustevatn, the Hardangerjøkulen glacier and the Hallingskarvet mountains. Aarhus's parents, Kristin Danielsen and Ruth Mjøen, asked their son to build a new cabin in this beautiful but challenging setting.

'The brief was to make the new building all about the view,' Aarhus says. 'In the living room, the idea was to create the experience of being outside, exposed to the constantly changing scenery, with the entire view-facing wall made of glass, along with an angled ceiling to "explode" the room even more. The tilted ceiling and the open wall are references to the *gapahuk*, a type of improvised shelter used by hikers, which has one side open to the elements.'

Building the house offered a number of challenges, with most of the materials flown to site by helicopter. To preserve the natural integrity of the land, Aarhus used a set of slim pillars bound to the bedrock to support the building on the hillside. The majority of the structure itself is made from Kebony pine, a specially treated, durable softwood that can withstand the seasonal extremes of the mountains. The house was flown in as a kit of parts, and largely assembled in just a few days within the narrow construction window during the summer.

The interiors also make extensive use of pine, with many built-in and bespoke elements, from seating to storage. The main living space, facing the open vista, is largely open plan, with areas for seating and dining, as well as a galley kitchen to the rear. A bedroom and bathroom at the far end are complemented by additional sleeping space in a mezzanine loft; in total, the cabin can sleep a dozen people. Despite the logistical constraints, it has a highly crafted and sculptural quality, while respecting its surroundings.

'We really appreciate how the landscape around the building has been so well preserved,' say Kristin and Ruth. 'We feel that we are truly in the middle of the wild.'

Rural Cabins   Cabin Ustaoset

Making extensive use of pine and stone, the interiors have a crafted and organic quality in keeping with the natural beauty of the surrounding landscape.

Rural Cabins

Cabin Ustaoset

'The brief was to
make the new cabin
all about the view.
In the living room, the
idea was to create the
experience of being
outside, exposed
to the constantly
changing scenery.'

The cabin floats upon a set of modest piloti, which help minimize disturbance to the site; the projecting roofline offers shelter to a porch alongside the front door.

Rural Cabins   Cabin Ustaoset

Gotland Summerhouse

Gotland, Sweden

Enflo Arkitekter & DEVE Architects

Resting in the Baltic Sea, 90 km (56 miles) from the mainland, Gotland is the largest of Sweden's many islands. Along with tourism and fishing, agriculture is one of the main 'industries', and the traditional barns and farmhouses of the isle provided a particular source of inspiration for the design of this modern summerhouse designed by Jens Enflo, in collaboration with Morten Vedelsbøl of DEVE Architects.

'The brief was to create a simple holiday home, as well as a guest house,' say Enflo and Vedelsbøl. 'Because the clients wanted to use local materials as much as possible and a simple construction method that could be managed by a local carpenter, we designed the building as a long extrusion of the archetypal Gotland barn profile, with a summer residence at one end and guest quarters at the other.'

The setting is verdant and sublime. There are open fields to the north, low forest to the south and sea views to the east. The pastoral surroundings and open landscape make the idea of a contemporary barn-style building all the more appropriate, while allowing the crisp profile of the building to stand out vividly. The timber framework is sourced from nearby, as is the pine for the façade, roof and interior joinery, and the exterior woodwork is stained with a tar-based treatment in the manner of the area's agricultural sheds and barns. By combining all of the elements beneath the pitched roofline of one building, the architects were able to retain a simple, pleasing form.

Family accommodation, comprising two bedrooms and a bathroom, is situated at one end, with a more central and open-plan living area warmed by a wood-burning stove. A guest suite sits at the opposite end of the building, allowing visitors a degree of independence and privacy. Between these two units is a sheltered breezeway, a flexible indoor–outdoor space suited to all kinds of weather. Vast sliding louvred panels – like a punctured barn door – sit to either side of this halfway zone. When closed, they still allow light and air to pass through, enhancing the level of protection from the elements and providing added security when the house is not in use. When the panels slide back, the space becomes a veranda, looking out across the pasture.

'We love the sense of connection between inside and out,' say the clients. 'The light here is very special, and the wildlife cannot be found anywhere else in Sweden. We have always enjoyed that outside space between the main part of the building and the guest house the most.'

A substantial, sheltered breezeway sits within the outline of the 'barn house', blurring the line between inside and outside living space.

The simple outline of the building, with its blackened timber coat, forms a sculptural presence in the open landscape, while the breezeway creates a contradiction between mass and transparency.

Rural Cabins

Gotland Summerhouse

Gudbrandslie Cabin

Tyinkrysset, Norway

Helen & Hard

The rugged mountain topography and extreme conditions of the surroundings helped to shape the design of this contemporary cabin near Tyinkrysset in central Norway. The alpine landscape here, close to the Jotunheimen National Park, is punctuated by lakes and deep valleys, and plays host to a number of ski centres and winter resorts. The clients asked architects Helen & Hard to design a mountain lodge that would include plenty of storage space for sports equipment, dedicated spaces for their children and strong connections with the landscape, while also preserving privacy. Otherwise, they were open to ideas and granted the team a significant degree of freedom to create an original home.

'The situation on the bare mountain means that the elements are very present,' explains architect Karen Jansen. 'The weather conditions can be quite rough, so we had to consider both significant snow loads and harsh winds during the design process. The geometry of the building echoes the landscape and has no straight angles, which was a challenge when it came to assembly on site.'

A parking garage, sauna and storage room for ski equipment were placed at basement level, along with other services, and this concrete-walled, semi-subterranean zone was pushed into the hillside, well protected from the elements. The main living spaces sit above on the upper level, which was constructed using spruce for the interiors and a heavy-duty Kebony cladding for the exterior. The green roof is planted with sedum. Much of the structural fabric of the house was prefabricated and assembled on site, speeding up construction time in the limited construction window available during the summer.

The accumulated snowfall means that over the course of the winter only the timber-clad upper storey of the cabin emerges from the snow. The living spaces here are arranged across a number of different floor levels, reflecting the shifting topography of the mountain and complemented by irregular windows that frame specific vistas and connect with an outdoor deck and terrace. The changes in floor level also allow for a greater sense of distinction between the main living spaces at the uppermost point of the building, with the master suite alongside. Bedrooms for the children are located a little lower on the gradient of the house and hill, to a difference of six steps.

The house exhibits a particular sensitivity to the landscape. Along with the green roof, the building has a geothermal heating system, which provides a regular and comfortable temperature within the home. The use of natural timber also helps to provide a healthier climate, regulating humidity. 'It's a robust refuge, integrated with the terrain,' Jansen continues. 'The house opens out to the south and west, while turning its back on the access road and neighbouring cabins, making you feel that you are all by yourself on the mountain, overlooking the fantastic natural surroundings.'

Rural Cabins   Gudbrandslie Cabin

The shifting levels of the main floor echo the rugged topography of the mountain setting, while also helping to distinguish the various different living spaces within the home.

During the winter months, only the timber-clad upper layer of the house is clearly visible, with the lower level largely disappearing into the mountain slope.

Hytte Hvasser

Hvasser, Norway

Hille Strandskogen Architects

This modestly scaled and sensitively conceived summer home on the Norwegian coast was designed to make the lightest of impressions upon the landscape. The land itself – around two hours south of Oslo and overlooking the straits that feed into the capital – had already belonged to client Annelise Thorbjørnsen's family for many years. Her grandparents had bought a farmstead here in the 1930s, and two decades later her parents built a small house, where she spent part of her childhood, developing a strong connection with the area. Eventually, the family recognized that the old cabin was in poor condition and would need to be replaced.

Thorbjørnsen and her partner, forester Trygve Refsdal, turned to architect Henrik Hille, who also has connections to the region, of the Oslo-based practice Hille Strandskogen. The beauty of the landscape implied a certain responsibility to create something that rested gently within it – a responsibility reinforced by planning restrictions on both the scale of the house and its position in relation to the protected coastline. Taking inspiration from the farmhouses and agricultural sheds of the region, Hille designed an L-shaped home in two parts, with an entrance zone between them and verandas for each, providing sheltered retreats facing the grass 'courtyard' on the windless side of the cabin.

Together, these elegant timber-clad structures have the look of a modern farmstead. The two-storey master building holds the main living spaces, arranged around a central fireplace, with the master bedroom suite alongside; a study and an additional bedroom are positioned on the upper level. The adjacent smaller 'barn' holds two guest bedrooms, creating a degree of privacy and independence for visiting friends. The choice of organic, natural materials helps tie the house to its rugged, rural setting. Although the building sits on a concrete base, the principal material is timber, with red-cedar cladding that will silver over time, pine for the framework and a combination of pine and ash for the interior joinery. When the house is not in use, the shutters are closed, reinforcing the simplicity of the architectural forms.

'The shutters function as a sun shield when they are open, and protect against wind and rain when closed,' Hille says. 'When they are closed, the cabin does have these associations with the old barns and boathouses of the area. This sense of simplicity in design and function was what we wanted to achieve from the beginning of the design process.'

Rural Cabins

Hytte Hvasser

Hytte Hvasser

Cedar shutters drop down to help protect the cabin when it is not in use, lending the house the simple outline of a timber barn sitting in the rugged, open landscape.

Villa Bureső

Slangerup, Denmark

Mette Lange Architects

Situated between the waters of Lake Bureső and a gentle, wooded landscape, this contemporary summerhouse by architect Mette Lange is immersed in nature. It is positioned with great sensitivity, sitting low in its site and featuring a green roof, planted with sedum, which allows the building to blur into the soft backdrop formed by the hillside. Built for a designer and a chef, along with their two children, the cabin is located in a rural part of Denmark, northwest of Copenhagen – about an hour away – and south of the historic town of Hillerød. Although dubbed a 'summerhouse', the villa is used for holidays and at weekends throughout the year.

'The location at the foot of the hill and right next to the lake creates this magical intimacy between the cabin and its surroundings,' Lange explains. 'It is a small, delicate wooden box, with an intimate sense of connection with nature. It is absolutely Scandinavian in everything, including the lives that are lived within its walls.'

The clients had bought the land in 2001, complete with two existing cabins, one of which has been restored to form a small guest house. The couple waited for some time before finally deciding to replace the main house with a new home, facing the lake. The plan subverts the idea of a rectangular, flat-roofed cabin in subtle but distinctive ways. Front and rear verandas are contained within the outline of the house, at opposite corners, while a brick chimney protrudes from one end. Three modest bedrooms – with the feel of a ship's berth – are pushed to the back, along with a single bathroom. A long, angled skylight helps draw additional sunlight into this portion of the house.

The main living space, facing the waters of the lake, is entirely open plan, comprising a kitchen and dining area, plus a seating zone arranged around the brick hearth, which has been painted a crisp white. Cedar was used for the exterior cladding, while the internal timber floors are from Danish flooring company Dinesen. Banks of sliding-glass windows at the front of the house both frame the views of the lake and help to dissolve the line between the building and the green lawn beyond, which forms an open courtyard.

'It is such a small house,' the clients note, 'so it feels just like one great, open space. The atmosphere is wonderful, and having the lake so close to the cabin makes it feel even more unique and special.'

Rural Cabins   Villa Buresø

The main living spaces are fluid and open, connecting with the gardens and the outdoor rooms alongside. Sleeping berths are arranged to the rear of the building.

Rural Cabins   Villa Buresø

Österklint 20

Bungenäs, Sweden

Skälsö Arkitekter

The island of Gotland, floating in the Baltic Sea between Sweden and Latvia, has its own distinct character and dialect, serving as home to around 60,000 people, many of whom live in the provincial capital of Visby. The Bungenäs peninsula sits to the north of the island, near the crossing point to the satellite island of Farö. It is a place of fascination, but not of particular beauty in the picture-book sense of the term, having first been ravaged by quarrying (for limestone) and then used as a series of military bases and defensive bunkers in the 1960s. When the army moved on, they left a curious mixture of rugged coastline and an almost post-industrial landscape, which is slowly being reclaimed by nature.

The area's unique character has attracted a particular kind of settler, drawn by the enigmatic setting. Architects Joel Phersson and Erik Gardell have designed a series of residences here, both new buildings and structures that have been creatively reused, incorporating some of the old bunkers. Österklint 20 is one of the most delightful of these, providing a new holiday home facing the sea. To the rear of the site, the old quarry wall forms a protective boundary, while the house itself comprises a handful of semi-separate micro-cabins, punctuated by complementary outdoor spaces and courtyards, and sheltered by a combination of timber walls and the rock face of the quarry behind. The topography of the site dictated the oblong formation of the building, which floats on a mixture of concrete slabs and supporting pillars.

A key part of the programme was to create a house that offered flexibility in how it might be used by the clients and visiting family and friends, with the possibility of opening up or closing down different sections. The compound nature of the house offers a fluid spatial experience, as one steps from inside to outside many times over within a building that is primarily used in the summer. The largest, central building holds the main living spaces, plus a bedroom annexe, while the two pavilions at each end of the rectangular site contain further bedrooms. For visits beyond the summer season, the focus is largely on the central section, heated by two wood-burning stoves, while the pavilions often remain closed.

'We found inspiration in the coastal houses of Gotland,' Phersson says, 'but most of all in the small, traditional fishermen's huts. The idea was to create private spaces that could easily be transformed into social and accessible ones. The house is quite characteristically Scandinavian in that it is modest in terms of scale and expression.'

Rural Cabins   Österklint 20

The rustic interiors are characterized by a modern simplicity and organic palette of materials. Carefully positioned windows frame key views of the coast.

The modular house is composed of a master
pavilion and a series of satellite structures,
with a sheltered courtyard forming both
a linking zone and an outdoor room.

The house was designed with flexibility in mind. The satellite pavilions can be brought into use or closed down with shutters according to need, and the courtyard protected and secured with a sliding gate.

Bjellandsbu-Åkrafjorden Cabin

Etne, Norway

Snøhetta

This modest rural cabin was designed to blend into a remote mountain landscape. Made of timber and stone, with a grass roof, from a distance it has the look of a natural feature set within the epic panorama. In the winter months, the building disappears completely under layers of snow. 'The roof is like a part of the earth lifted up, with the cabin tucked underneath,' says architect Margrethe Lund. 'The mountain terrain has few traces of civilization, so we thought that the cabin should appear secondary to the landscape. Nature itself shaped the building, but the cabin barely affects it. The footprint was kept to a minimum, and the building process had very little impact.'

The client, Osvald Bjelland, had a particular spot in mind, some distance from his family farm, which sits in the mountains of Hordaland and within the sparsely populated municipality of Etne. Situated to the south of Bergen, this is where the mountains meet the coastal fjords, with the area home to the Folgefonna National Park and a number of nature reserves. The remoteness of the location means that the area is accessible only on foot or on horseback, by snow scooter or by helicopter, which was how most of the materials were brought to the site.

The opportunities to build here are carefully controlled, with cabins and hunting lodges restricted to a size of no more than 35 m² (377 sq ft). Having chosen a beautiful site close to a mountain lake, Bjelland requested a cabin that could – at a squeeze – accommodate a party of 21 hikers. 'The cabin realizes a family dream, held over many generations and many years, for a shelter at this exact spot,' he explains. 'I love its design and relationship to nature, as well as its humble yet majestic personality.'

The building was created with a steel frame, with steel also used for the chimney, but the rest of the materials are organic. The rounded form of the house appears like a small hillock, with the grass roof helping to disguise it even further. To one side, a wall of glass frames a view of the lake and the mountain landscape, while a triptych of small, irregular windows sits within the timber façade on the other side of the lodge.

Inside, the cabin is essentially one open room, arranged around the central fireplace, which functions like a campfire. Timber-framed banquettes and sleeping platforms surround the hearth, while the rounded shape of the roof offers a reassuring feeling of shelter and enclosure. Fully self-sufficient and off-grid, the house is heated by the fireplace. Although gas is used for cooking at the small kitchenette, water comes from the lake and an outdoor toilet is hidden in the landscape nearby.

'We wanted the cabin to be respectful of the landscape and to use natural materials,' Lund adds. 'It has more in common with traditional Norwegian building than with Scandinavian modernist architecture, but is still highly modern in its shape.'

Rural Cabins

Bjellandsbu-Åkrafjorden Cabin

The micro-cabin comprises one room, arranged around a central hearth. Built-in seating also serves as beds, complemented by mezzanine sleeping platforms.

Rural Cabins

Bjellandsbu-Åkrafjorden Cabin

The modest dwelling vanishes into the folds of the landscape, becoming almost invisible from a distance. In winter, the hut disappears under the snow.

Arctic Treehouse Hotel

Rovaniemi, Finland

Studio Puisto

Situated along the Arctic Circle and in the heart of Lapland, the Arctic Treehouse Hotel caters to tourists attracted by the Northern Lights and Santa Claus. The region is also rich in wildlife and ski resorts, while the nearby city of Rovaniemi boasts three buildings designed by Alvar Aalto. For a forested site not far from the city, the firm Studio Puisto was commissioned to design a new kind of hotel with a direct and vivid sense of connection to nature. The result is a series of floating cabins, raised on stilts and coated in timber shingles, perched among the pine trees and located on a gently sloping hillside.

'Everything in the design process started from the natural environment of the Arctic and how visitors will experience it,' says architect Willem van Bolderen, who worked on the project with colleagues Emma Johansson and Mikko Jakonen. 'The contrast between this wild landscape and these safe, nest-like spaces has been a guiding element. The wooden shingles were inspired by the surrounding forest, but they also make the cabins look a little like traditional Finnish toy cows, made from pine cones.'

There is certainly something of a zoomorphic quality to the stilted cabins, which can look frozen in time to a guest walking through the woods. Green roofs help the buildings disappear into the greenery of the trees and compensate for any disturbance to the ground below. The architects and their clients were both, in any case, intent on a light touch. The team was commissioned to create 32 cabins in all, as well as the on-site restaurant. The cabins are placed among the trees, parallel to one another, or, in some cases, as conjoined twins, with a linking door allowing larger families or groups to use two cabins as a combined holiday home.

The entrances to the cabins are at ground level on the upper portion of the hill, while supporting pillars keep the structures level as they push out above the sloping gradient. Service spaces such as the kitchenette, shower room and storage are arranged around the entrance hallway to the rear, with the cabins opening out to a combined lounge/bedroom. The key moment of the design is the floor-to-ceiling window, which frames a view of the surrounding forest and, with its elevated position, gives the impression of a floating treehouse, suspended above the gradient of the hillside.

As part of the focus on sustainability, many elements of the cabin were prefabricated and then lifted into position, minimizing the impact on the environment and limiting the construction period. The buildings sit well within the tradition of warm, organic 'soft' modernism established by Aalto and others. 'Using wood as the main material when building in the forest is particularly Scandinavian,' Van Bolderen continues. 'Although we have kept the detailing quite minimal, it retains a sense of character through the use of these pure materials.'

Rural Cabins   Arctic Treehouse Hotel

The sleeping spaces face a floor-to-ceiling picture window, which frames a view of the forest beyond. The elevated position of the cabins gives them a treehouse quality.

Rural Cabins   Arctic Treehouse Hotel

Coated in wooden shingles and supported by piloti, the cabins form a 'herd' of carefully positioned structures within the woods, which stand out all the more in the snow.

Rural Cabins

Arctic Treehouse Hotel

Archipelago House

Husarö, Sweden

Tham & Videgård

The architectural firm of Tham & Videgård has reinvented and updated the cabin typology in the form of Archipelago House, located on the Swedish island of Husarö. The team describes the house as a 'platform for living', with the building arranged on one level and unified by a single roof-turned-canopy, which protects and shelters the inside and outside spaces beneath it. Elevated a step above the ground on supporting pillars, the platform has a unity that recalls a pontoon or houseboat, an impression reinforced by the island setting and proximity to the shore.

Husarö sits among the thousands of small islands within the Stockholm archipelago to the east of the city. For centuries the island served as a home to marine pilots, who helped guide shipping through the maze of islands, and is now accessible by ferry with a journey time of around two and a half hours from the city. All of the materials needed to build the new cabin were brought in by boat, with the choice of timber meeting the requirement for a lightweight material, as well as linking back to traditional methods of construction.

'Since the 17th century the building method of these islands has been in timber,' explains architect Bolle Tham. 'The house continues that tradition, as well as relating to a specific place in a direct way, adjusting the plan to accommodate existing boulders on the site and designing the façades so that they stand out against the bark of the mature pines.'

Initially, the clients wanted a family cabin, plus a guest house, but ultimately the separate elements were brought together in one building. The roof and floor plate have the shape of a rhomboid, while a series of spaces sit between them in a zigzag formation, complemented by a substantial veranda. A sequence of three interconnecting spaces form the heart of the house – the master bedroom, central living room and a combined kitchen/dining area and studio – all of which filter out to the adjoining terrace via sliding walls of glass, blurring the boundaries between inside and out. Smaller spaces and service zones are pushed to the rear of the house, including a children's bunkroom, a bathroom/laundry area and guest bedrooms.

The outer fabric of the house comprises an abstract but crafted shingle façade, made from a framework of pine and plywood boards, stained black. Around the veranda, the side wall and roof have been punctured to form a louvred screen allowing for partial shade and shelter. There is a purposeful contrast between the dark geometry of the exterior of the cabin and the light palette of the interiors, where the tongue-and-groove walls and much of the fitted furniture are painted white, while the oak floors have been oiled to give a lighter finish. As well as using renewable materials, the cabin features natural ventilation and is heated in the winter months by a wood-burning stove.

'The house both blends in with its surroundings and stands out as a new type of house, in relation to the old farm buildings and fishermen's huts,' Tham continues. 'The layout helps to create a series of outdoor spaces that are sheltered from the island's strong winds, while the reflections and mirror-like effect of the large panes of glass create a quality in which nature, space and the horizon all interact together.'

Rural Cabins   Archipelago House

The kitchen and sitting room sit at the centre of the house, in a staggered sequence of spaces that also includes the master bedroom. All of these key zones flow out to the semi-sheltered veranda.

Rural Cabins

Archipelago House

The entire cabin sits on a platform hovering just above the ground. This platform – and the roof canopy, which mirrors it – hold and protect the internal living spaces and the outdoor rooms that adjoin them.

Cabin Vindheim

Sjoga, Norway

Vardehaugen

Architect Håkon Matre Aasarød of Norwegian firm Vardehaugen has explored the theme of the 21st-century cabin through a series of projects, experimenting with form, geometry and intersecting volumes. These houses have also been infused with the essential characteristics of the cabin, such as modesty of scale, lightness of touch and timber construction. Cabin Vindheim offers a continuation of these explorations, within a building at the heart of the forest that both surprises and delights.

It sits deep in a forested area within the alpine landscape of Sjoga, which lies to the north of Oslo and west of the Oppland town of Lillehammer, well known as a ski resort and host of the 1994 Winter Olympics. The location is remote, with no services, with the greenery of the spruce trees forming a verdant backdrop for much of the year, while layers of snow blanket the region in winter, when the temperature can drop to -20° C (-4° F).

'My main inspiration for the project was the classic motif of a snowbound cabin, with the roof protruding from the snow,' says Aasarød, who was a founding partner at Fantastic Norway Architects before establishing his own practice. 'I have always been fascinated by the way snow blurs the border between nature and architecture, so we explored this idea through the concept of an extended roof, which connects the building to the landscape, like a rock sticking up from the ground.'

The roofline of the cabin – commissioned by Brita Hjelmseth and Vetle Vindheim – is composed of a series of intersecting diagonals with an abstract, geometric pattern, with the lower points of each touching the earth. The exterior, including the roof, is coated in ore pine and stained black,

reinforcing the outline and composition of the cabin and lending it, as Aasarød notes, 'weight and presence'. Against the white of the winter snows, the black abstraction of the house becomes accentuated and intense. At the heart of the single-storey cabin is a central living area, complete with a wood-burning stove, which includes the kitchen, dining area and seating zone. Bedrooms, a bathroom and service spaces are situated to either side, complemented by adjoining terraces. For the interiors, the key material is a waxed poplar veneer, which has a lightness enhanced by extensive glazing and skylights and provides an organic warmth that contrasts with the black façade.

The house is fully off-grid, with heating from the wall-mounted stove and electricity from solar panels, while water is pumped by hand from a well and stored in the technical room of the cabin. In the winter months, the setting offers a powerful sense of isolation and escape within the depths of the forest. 'The trees transform into enormous white sculptures and the atmosphere is magical,' Aasarød says. 'It's so quiet that you can hear the footsteps of a squirrel or snow falling off a branch. While listening to the silence of the landscape, you can appreciate why local folklore is filled with mystical stories from the deep forest.'

Rural Cabins

Cabin Vindheim

The neutral, natural palette of the interiors offers a vivid contrast to the crisp, black silhouette of the exterior. In the main living area, an integrated wood-burner forms part of a portfolio of solutions for off-grid living.

The irregular geometry of the façade, with its black-stained timber cladding, stands out vividly against the winter forest. Intersecting diagonals provide an abstraction that brings modernity to a familiar typology.

Åre Solbringen

Åre, Sweden

Waldemarson Berglund Arkitekter

The mountain of Åre and its eponymous town form one of Scandinavia's most prestigious ski resorts, with its wide range of runs, including pistes for downhill racing, and over 30 lifts. Tourists began arriving following the construction of a railway line in the 1880s, and by the mid-1950s the town was hosting the Alpine World Championships. Given the topography of the region and the importance of winter sports, it seems only appropriate that both helped to inspire the design of three new cabins by architects Jonas Waldemarson and Paulina Berglund.

'Since being on the slopes is one of the conditions for skiing, it was tempting to have the buildings do something similar – or at least give that impression,' says Waldemarson. 'We decided to design a series of houses that would sit on the ground without disturbing the mountain, in which all of the rooms would have generous height and windows with a view. As this idea fitted perfectly with local planning regulations, it only remained for us to discover if it would be possible to create a workable and interesting plan for these sloping cabins.'

Many traditional homes here are pushed into the hillside, with dark and semi-subterranean basement levels, while construction guidelines insist that even new houses are built in the direction of the slope, with the façades facing outwards. The architects were asked to design a triptych of cabins on the outskirts of the town on a south-facing slope, looking across the river and out to the mountains beyond. Embracing the challenge imposed by the planning restrictions, they placed the cabins in an almost parallel formation running down the slope, following its gradient, like three skis laid upon the mountain.

The cabins were constructed with wood frames resting upon slim brick pillars. These floating buildings were then clad in timber panels and highly insulated, with oak floors and plasterboard wall finishing within; the wood for the project was sourced locally. A circulation axis sits to one side, providing a sequence of steps that links five different levels, as the buildings flow down the gradient of the slope. Entrances and service spaces are to the rear, followed by bedrooms, a bathroom and sauna, a kitchen/dining room, and finally a living room that faces outwards to the view, complete with floor-to-ceiling glass connecting with a projecting terrace, which emerges from each building as a cantilevered lip. A sequence of windows ensures that each space has natural light and views.

'When you first see the houses, they may seem odd or surprising in the surrounding context,' Waldemarson explains. 'But as soon as you come closer, you begin to understand why they are designed the way that they are. They make perfect and logical sense and add something extra to the area.'

Rural Cabins   Åre Solbringen

The interiors step down the hillside by degrees via a long stairway to one side. The run of spaces culminates in the kitchen/ dining area overlooking the main sitting room, with a fireplace and floor-to-ceiling glass connecting with the views.

Rural Cabins   Åre Solbringen

Coastal Retreats

So much of the identity of Scandinavia is rooted in its relationship to the sea and its waterways. The coastline is both epic and extraordinary, with glacial fjords and archipelagos, and the Nordic countries are truly blessed when it comes to geological splendours. Bordered by the Baltic, Norwegian, Barents and North seas, Scandinavia's gulfs and sea lanes form vital trade routes and fishing grounds, while the deep waters play an essential part in the history, culture and mythology of the region. The coast, like the forests and mountains, forms one of the principal landscapes, a place of endless opportunities and enthralling experiences.

The notion of an island escape has particular resonance for the residents of the Nordic countries, for whom a sense of connection to water is both familiar and natural. The tradition of a seaside cabin runs deep, while familial relationships with one part of the coast or another run through the generations. For contemporary architects and their clients, the notion of such a retreat still has a profound allure.

'The summerhouse, or *fritidshus*, as it is known in Swedish, is a typically Scandinavian typology,' notes architect Mats Fahlander. 'Many were built during the 1950s and '60s. They have a special connection to nature, which is perceived as something soothing, rather than threatening. This connection is informed by a long tradition of *allemansrätt*, which ensures that everyone is allowed to roam freely, provided nothing is disturbed.'

Many of the coastal houses featured in this chapter sit in striking or startling locations, often quite remote, where the experience of the natural world is immediate and sometimes raw. In some cases these houses have already been in the same family for a number of generations, and a new summerhouse or cabin is a replacement for a previous house brought low by the elements, or an addition to a family enclave. In any event, they tend to be homes of great modesty and limited scale. Planning restrictions across the region generally limit the height and footprint of coastal homes, particularly in areas of natural beauty or environmental sensitivity. New buildings are conceived and placed with particular care, reducing overall visibility and impact upon their surroundings.

There is an essential respect among Nordic architects for the beauty of nature, with the idea that a site should be preserved and protected as far as possible. A repeated idea is that these summerhouses and coastal cabins should touch the ground as lightly as possible, to the extent that they could be removed at the end of their lives, leaving behind only the most minimal impression on nature. This was certainly true of Fahlander's own summerhouse on the coast of Bohuslän, in western Sweden (p. 92). 'Great care was put into the relationship between the house and its surroundings,' he says. 'It hovers above the ground, and it is possible to walk around it on an outdoor bridge, which floats above the rocks. The construction phase was not allowed to have any lasting impact on the surrounding landscape, and the house has the potential to be removed in the future without leaving any trace.'

A similar approach helps define other coastal houses, from Kolman Boye Architects' Vega Hytte (p. 124), located on the Norwegian island of Vega, to Lund Hagem's escapist home on another Norwegian island, Lille Arøya (p. 130), which floats above the rocks and rock pools, suspended on a platform for living by slender steel legs. The choice of materials tends to be organic in nature, with timber commonly used, but there is also a recognition that these are extreme and demanding settings in which to build a house. Coastal winds and saltwater spray take a heavy toll on any building, in much the same way as they would on a boat or a ship. Architects have taken many pointers from boat-building and maritime engineering, as they seek ways of mitigating the impact of such an extreme environment and ensure that their cabins and summerhouses are as robust and low maintenance as possible.

Weekend House, designed by architect Knut Hjeltnes for a tiny host island near Herøy, in Norway (p. 120), certainly owes much to boat-building traditions. The steel-framed building, with inner and outer skins, as well as a waterproofed technical room for services, was largely constructed on a nearby island and then lifted out by sea crane to its awaiting plinth. Norwegian firm Jarmund/ Vigsnæs used a reflective metal coat for the exterior of their Aluminium Cabin (p. 108) on the country's western coast. Like Fahlander's and Hjeltnes's projects, the structure has a nautical influence.

Although the material – aluminium – is far from organic, the building's shell reflects the landscape, sky and sea, helping to lessen the visual impact of the house. Such houses are not only bases for family experiences and enjoying the pleasures of the sea – fishing, canoeing, sailing, swimming, and so on – but also for appreciating nature itself. They become belvederes and lookout stations, observatories and hides. Part of the brief for these retreats is that they should connect to the outdoors and to the sea in an immediate way that heightens the experiential quality of both. The successes in meeting such a challenge make these coastal houses stand apart.

Slävik Summerhouse

Lysekil, Sweden

Mats Fahlander

The coastline of Bohuslän, on Sweden's western shore, is one of the country's great wilderness areas. It is populated by thousands of small islands and indented with countless inlets and coves, as well as the open mouths of the Götaland fjords. This area of rugged beauty has fascinated architect Mats Fahlander since spending summer holidays here as a child. The same was true of the client who, years later, commissioned Fahlander to build a summerhouse in the same location.

'For many generations, members of a large, extended family have spent their summers here,' Fahlander explains. 'There are no visible boundaries and the sea and the countryside are the main attractions. As the family grew, more houses were built. This particular house was built for one of the sons on a high point on the rocks, with room for family and guests. The site is immersed in nature, surrounded by the sea, granite rocks and windswept trees.'

Although the coastal setting is enchanting, it also made the location – with its saltwater spray and biting winds – a challenging spot in which to build. Fahlander points out that the environment here is so extreme that the nearby island of Malmön is used by the construction industry as a place for testing the durability of its products. His client, who is an old friend, wanted a compact summerhouse that would be low maintenance, representing a substantial challenge in this harsh context.

Wishing to preserve the integrity of the rocky site as far as possible, Fahlander decided to raise the building above the ground on slender piloti, creating a floating platform, rather like a pontoon. Two barrel-vaulted roofs, resembling a conjoined pair of upturned hulls, adds to the building's boat-like quality. The framework is timber but, keeping the coastal conditions in mind, Fahlander clad the house in cement fibre board. It is modest in scale at 90 m² (970 sq ft), while a small guest house and sauna alongside adds another 28 m² (300 sq ft) to the overall programme, forming a subservient echo of the main cabin.

The house is split into two distinct halves. One side contains an open-plan living space, with extensive glazing facing the sea views, while the other holds two bedrooms and services, as well as an entry hallway. The entire building is bordered by a walkway, like a ship's deck, while additional decks and seating areas are tucked into the rocks nearby, with heavy-duty galvanized steel used for the balconies and other exposed detailing. Within, the interior joinery and wall panelling are made from untreated fir, and a wood-burning stove provides heat.

'To sit down in the living room overlooking the sea on a stormy day is a wonderful experience, rather like sitting in the cockpit of a plane,' says Fahlander. 'From the outside, the summerhouse becomes glowing and golden, with the wooden panels inside set alight by the low, setting sun.'

Floor-to-ceiling glass windows at the front of the house slide back to create an immediate connection with the outdoors. The open-plan living space forms one half of the cabin.

The house, with its twin vaulted roofs, floats
on an elevated platform; spaces among the
rocks nearby have been colonized as open-air
seating and dining areas.

Folded Roof House

Claesson Koivisto Rune

The growing interest in prefabricated homes over recent years sits in synergy with the increasing sophistication of the architectural designs of the buildings themselves. Prefabricating component parts in a factory helps to reduce the costs of constructing a home, as well as the amount of time and energy spent on site, compared with traditional building methods. In the Nordic countries, in particular, where settings can be challenging and extreme, with small seasonal windows for construction, the concept has particular appeal.

Swedish architectural firm Claesson Koivisto Rune joined forces with prefabrication specialists Arkitekthus to create a timber-framed and -clad home that offers a modern reinterpretation of the Nordic cabin. The single-storey building has bedrooms and bathrooms at either end and an open-plan living area at the centre, featuring an extensive sequence of glazing and glass doors that leads out onto a timber deck. The architects subverted the traditional rectangular format of a cabin by creating a fold, or tuck, in the zinc roof, which also holds hidden guttering and downpipes, simplifying the outline of the building.

The house is located on Muskö, one of the larger islands of the Stockholm archipelago, situated to the south of the city, and accessed by road bridges and a tunnel. The client was able to tailor the design somewhat, and requested an additional guest house plus a sauna nearby, as well as a jetty, all designed by the team. Sitting on the rocks and bordered by trees, the prefabricated building and its satellite structures manage to feel contextual. The main living spaces and deck face the vista of the Baltic waters, connecting with the coastscape.

'The weathered wood and grey roof are the exact colour of the bare granite the house sits on,' explains architect Mårten Claesson. 'The geometry of the building is also a kind of interpretation of the surrounding rock. The house is "normal with a twist" – a rectangular box with an off-angled, inverted peak mid-roof. It is subtle, but gives the building a lot of character.'

Folded Roof House is the team's second design for Arkitekthus (the first is a two-storey design called Plus House, p. 228). Other Swedish architects featured in this prefabricated portfolio include Thomas Sandell, Wingårdh Arkitektkontor (p. 208) and Tham & Videgård (pp. 72, 156) .

Coastal Retreats   Folded Roof House

The main living spaces sit at the centre of the house, in an open-plan zone that connects with the veranda and the coastal views, with bedrooms and bathrooms positioned to either side.

The architects also designed a small guest house in a sympathetic style, along with a sauna close to the jetty. Together with the main cabin, the buildings form a triptych of modest structures in the landscape.

Aluminium Cabin

Nøtterøy, Norway

Jarmund/Vigsnæs Arkitekter

The owners of this striking modern home on the western coast of Norway call it the 'Sardinen', a nickname that picks up on the house's unique appearance, with its aluminium skin that reflects the rocks, trees and sky. But it also references the history of the maritime surroundings and the sardine factory, or cannery, which used to operate just along the coastline here. The setting is certainly seductive, overlooking an extensive archipelago that sits within the open mouth of the Oslo fjord; the city itself is around 110 km (68 miles) to the north.

'The proximity to the sea and the opportunities for a life spent on boats make the location special to us,' say the owners, a retired high-school teacher and a lawyer with two grown-up children, who have another cabin of their own on a nearby island. 'It is a beautiful and untouched archipelago landscape with long, warm summers. We almost have a "midnight sun" from early June to late July, when it never gets entirely dark.'

The new building, known by the architects Jarmund/Vigsnæs as the Aluminium Cabin, replaces a small but dilapidated summerhouse that once stood upon the same site, overlooking the fjord. The modest scale and size of the new, single-storey house, which is 90 m² (970 sq ft), was partly dictated by planning restrictions, as well as by the desire to tuck the cabin into the topography of the rocky coastal landscape in as sensitive and discreet a manner as possible. At the same time, it needed to be able to withstand the salty conditions of the area, which can have an extreme impact on traditionally made buildings. This led to the idea of using seawater-resistant aluminium, whose mirror-like quality allows the house to disappear into the landscape.

'The connection between inside and out was important,' explains architect Alessandra Kosberg. 'The cabin consists of three, interconnected volumes, with outdoor terraces surrounding them. All three of these outdoor "rooms" offer options for sun and shelter throughout the day.'

A substantial living area, warmed by a wood-burning stove, features extensive walls of glass that open onto the adjoining terraces and face the views of the water. A small kitchen sits to the rear of the house, two guest bedrooms form the second volume and the master suite sits within a third, more private space at the other end of the main entrance zone. The rocks around the house help provide a degree of shelter and enclosure, while their sculptural mass contrasts with the open views of the fjord.

'From the inside, we like the stunning views and the light,' say the owners. 'From the outside, we love the special shape of the cabin and the changing colours of the façade, owing to the mirror-effect of the aluminium.'

Coastal Retreats   Aluminium Cabin

The relationship between inside and outside
space was a priority of the overall design,
which connects adjoining terraces and the
coastal vista.

The single-storey cabin is tucked discreetly
among the trees and rocks, while the
mirrored surface of the building reflects the
surroundings and blends into the landscape.

Coastal Retreats   Aluminium Cabin

Split House

Asker, Norway

Jarmund/Vigsnæs Arkitekter

The town of Asker rests on the shores of the inner Oslofjord, southwest of the Norwegian capital. Here, the waters of the fjord are broad and open, and form part of the extraordinary maritime hinterland between the open ocean and the city. Although new construction is tightly controlled along this extensive shoreline, the clients approached the architects at Jarmund/Vigsnæs with a site that offered a panoramic vista over the fjord. The design of the two-storey house emerged from the character and topography of the land and the wish to frame different vistas, leading to the idea of 'splitting' the façade of the house where it faces the water.

'We wanted to design a house that would spring out of the ground and feel quite humble to the rear, where there are neighbours, but with an extensive openness towards the sea,' explains Håkon Vigsnæs. 'But we also wanted to break down the scale of the house, so that it is not too dominant. The split allows for a variation of spatial qualities and breaks up the sense of scale towards the fjord.'

The house is pushed into the hillside, with a semi-submerged lower level holding services and bedrooms, plus a media room. This part of the building is clad in stone, helping to anchor the building in its setting, while a lightwell to the rear brings natural light into areas with limited connections to the outdoors. The upper level holds the principal living spaces, which benefit from their elevated position in terms of access to the views and light. A procession of entry spaces leads to the key elements of the split floorplan, with the main living room facing in one direction, complemented by an adjoining veranda, and an open-plan kitchen and dining area framing a subtly different panorama.

The upper level of the steel-framed building is clad in cedar, while the green roof is covered in sedum. The sculptural 'prows' of the split project outwards, lending the house a subtle nautical quality. The projecting veranda and dining zone have the feel of lookout stations, or coastal observatories, and offer a particularly vivid sense of connection with the broad waterway, punctuated by small islands and used by constant maritime traffic.

'We don't see our architecture as especially Scandinavian, but as site-orientated,' Vigsnæs adds, 'and, to some degree, focused on local traditions and craftsmanship. The idea of striving for views and light in our landscape and climate, however, might be considered Scandinavian.'

Coastal Retreats

Split House

The upper storey splays as it faces the fjord, with the kitchen and dining room to one side and the main living area to the other, each framing a different perspective of the water.

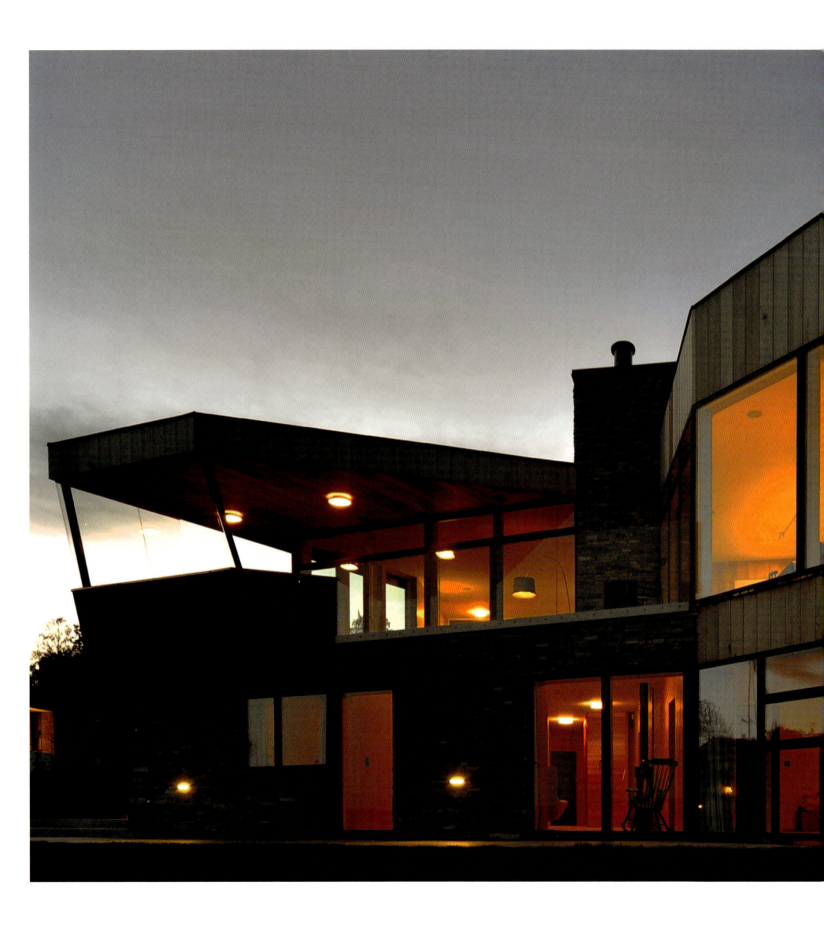

The house is pushed into a gentle slope, with the upper storey boasting a prominent, elevated position that makes the most of the views. This upper level is clad in timber, while the lower floor, pushed into the hillside, is covered in stone.

Weekend House

Sildegarnsholmen, Norway

Knut Hjeltnes Sivilarkitekter

In 1992, on the west coast of Norway, a powerful storm washed away an old fishermen's warehouse, leaving a vacant stone plinth. Many years later architect Knut Hjeltnes and his clients, Peter and Marianne Straume, saw this as an opportunity to fill the empty foundation with a new weekend home among the islands of Herøy, an escapist retreat where the couple and their two children could enjoy fishing and water sports, as well as hiking in the nearby mountains and entertaining friends.

'The most important requirement was a house that could resist the winter storms, but we also wanted the look and feel of a boathouse, something modern but practical inside,' says Peter Straume. 'As the climate can be harsh in this part of the country, we were not looking for a holiday home, but a year-round weekend base for a number of activities. Our wish was to combine a good indoor experience with the fantastic natural setting we have just outside, which we wanted to be part of the home.'

Designing and building a new house in this extreme setting offered a number of key challenges, from the difficulties in accessing the site to the very limited size of the island itself, which consists of little more than the stone plinth, a small patch of grassland and a spur of rock. 'We wanted to design a house that could withstand the harsh weather, in a way that would benefit the architecture,' Hjeltnes says. 'But we also needed to find a way to prefabricate the building on a larger island nearby, transport it as a nearly complete structure and lift it into place.'

The solutions employed by Hjeltnes and his team owe much to the example of boat-building. The house was constructed with a strong steel frame attached to a pre-

prepared concrete sole, or foot pad, and consists of a protective outer skin made from horizontal, weather-resistant Kebony timber boards, arranged in a horizontal lattice, so that any waves striking the building could easily drain away. The same timber is used for a series of 21 protective shutters and doorways that slide or fold. An inner hull of steel and glass offers another layer of protection, and services are contained in a watertight technical room, sealed with a ferry-style hatch.

The entire three-storey building was lifted by a sea crane and transported to its host island, where it was slotted into place on the stone plinth, which now has a small jetty and mooring pontoon alongside. The plan provides living spaces on the ground floor, including a porch within the overall outline of the house, which can also be protected by timber shutters when it is not in use. Steel-legged furniture and hanging stairways allow for the possibility of seawater occasionally making its way inside. Bedrooms are arranged at either end at first-floor level, while a substantial attic provides a flexible space for storage.

When the shutters are closed, the house assumes a pleasing simplicity of form that does, indeed, give the impression of a boathouse and echoes the original warehouse that stood on the site. At the same time, given the modesty and low-lying nature of the miniature island, it appears to sit upon the water in a magical way, so that it also resembles a floating houseboat.

Coastal Retreats   Weekend House

The design of the house draws inspiration from the look of vernacular boathouses. A series of protective timber shutters unfold and slide back to reveal the doorways and windows when the building is in use.

Coastal Retreats   Weekend House

Vega Hytte

Vega, Norway

Kolman Boye Architects

The rocky shoreline of the island of Vega is punctuated now and again by traditional fishermen's huts. These timber-framed sheds, or *nausta*, are raised up on wooden piers, clad in a mixture of wood or corrugated tin, and used for storing nets and fishing equipment. The simple huts, tucked into the coastline and weathered by the elements, have a discreet charm and formed one point of inspiration for the design of Vega Hytte, which sits among the rocks, overlooking the sea and the other islands of the Vega archipelago in western Norway, now listed as a Unesco World Heritage Site.

The cottage was commissioned by three siblings – Alexander, Joachim and Elisabeth Mørk-Eidem – who have a long-standing connection to the region. They wanted a modest holiday home that would sit gently in the landscape they loved and do as little harm to it as possible. Architects Victor Boye Julebæk and Erik Kolman Janouch embraced both the challenge and the setting, undertaking a number of fact-finding trips to the island and drawing inspiration from the rugged site and its surroundings.

'The family wanted a robust house that could withstand the harsh climate, accommodate the uneven terrain and become part of the landscape in an effortless manner,' Julebæk explains. 'To ensure that our design was in harmony with the site, we travelled to the island several times to study the positioning, access paths, views and heights. Each visit provided us with new insights and led to adjustments and alterations.'

Limited access to the site, along with the need to protect the surrounding landscape, meant that all materials had to be carried in from the nearby track by hand or transported via a pulley system. The principal material is timber, with larch for the cladding, Norwegian pine for the interior panels, ash for the floors and birch for joinery, such as doors and cabinets. The entire cabin floats on slender pillars that meet the uneven ground below with minimal disturbance, and was designed to be as low maintenance as possible. 'The project is defined by what could be called poetic pragmatism,' Julebæk adds. 'The house has a tranquil, natural and unpretentious quality. The complexity lies in the encounter between the landscape and the building, nature and culture.'

Rather like the huts by the shore, which often sit in pairs or triptychs, the cottage is formed from two adjoining parts, each framed by a pitched roof. This helps to lessen the scale and impact of the house, as well as define a sense of separation between the main, open-plan living area in one half of the cottage and the bedrooms, service zones and loft space in the other; a shift in floor level over a few steps reinforces the subtle sense of separation between communal and private space. Large picture windows frame the extraordinary views.

'The view of the sea and the mountains is unique,' says Alexander Mørk-Eidem, a theatre director. 'It's like having front-row seats to this dramatic scenery, where the rocky island meets the Atlantic. My favourite place is sitting by the fireplace and looking out over the ocean during a storm. The warmth and seclusion of it, together with the spectacular view, creates a very special feeling.'

Coastal Retreats

Vega Hytte

The main living spaces sit within one distinct volume of the house, while the bedrooms are in another, which includes the loft. The interiors feature a palette of natural materials, such as pine, ash and birch.

Characterized by 'poetic pragmatism', the cabin – partly inspired by traditional fishermen's huts – does its best to sit on the land as unobtrusively as possible.

Lille Arøya

Larvik, Norway

Lund Hagem Architects

There is an endearing lightness of touch to much contemporary Scandinavian architecture. Within precious coastal and rural landscapes, in particular, there is a desire to create buildings that have an almost temporary quality, as though they are simply guests – an ideal that suggests that one day the visiting building could disappear and hardly a trace of it would remain. This was very much the thinking behind the design and build of a new summerhouse on the island of Lille Arøya, one of a group of islands jostling for position along the coastline here.

Commissioned by Kaja Klingenberg and Alexander Westberg, the building sits lightly upon the rocky edge of an island southwest of Oslo and some distance to the west of the town of Larvik. This new family retreat replaces an older building nearby, and was regulated by a tight set of planning limitations on size and scale. 'For us to be allowed to replace the old building, the new one had to be both less visible and provide a positive solution,' explains architect Kristine Strøm-Gundersen. 'The client's key requirement was that the building connected in a better way to the landscape, and offered shelter from the prevailing southwesterly wind.'

The architects decided to embrace and protect the rugged, irregular site, creating a platform suspended over the rocks and pools below, anchored by a series of slim steel supports drilled directly into the stone, with spaces around and below the platform serving as boat moorings and shelters. The single-storey, timber-framed cabin, made with glulam beams, sits upon this 'floating' platform, which cantilevers out towards the water, and comprises three distinct elements. An accommodation wing holds a sequence of bedrooms and bathrooms, punctuated by walkthroughs and a breezeway. The main

living spaces are held in another section of the house, which projects outwards from the base rock, cross-braced by triangular tethers anchoring the elevated structure at each end. This part of the house is bordered with glass, forming a belvedere, or observatory, that looks out to the sea lanes and passing ships. The third element consists of the terraces and decks that sit on the platform between the two enclosed parts of the cabin, complete with integrated benches.

Owing to the isolated location of the house, materials were flown in by helicopter, including the concrete used in select parts of the cabin, such as the bathrooms. All of the materials were carefully selected to be able to withstand the extreme coastal conditions, from the fir for the cladding and floors to the brass for the flashings and detailing. The design of the crafted interiors was a collaboration between the architects and Klingenberg, who is herself a designer.

At high tide, the cabin assumes a floating, almost surreal quality, suspended within the folds of the rocks and inlets. 'It could be seen as a vernacular interpretation in the Scandinavian tradition, through its use and understanding of the surrounding landscape and materials,' Strøm-Gundersen notes. 'But I would add that the cabin is not so much a building as an exploration of the threshold between the natural and the manmade. It sits between land and water.'

The living spaces push out from the main body of the house, offering a glass-sided belvedere facing the open water, while also flowing freely out to the adjoining terrace.

The cabin sits on a platform hovering above the rocks and water pools, rather like a houseboat; the bedrooms are arranged in a line to the rear of the house.

Coastal Retreats   Lille Arøya

Stupet

Omberg, Sweden

Petra Gipp Arkitektur

The scale of Lake Vättern suggests an inland sea. This is the second-largest lake in Sweden, after neighbouring Lake Vänern, with an extraordinary 'coastline' that extends for over 600 km (373 miles). Surrounded by forests of pine and spruce, the lake provides the region with clean drinking water, which can be imbibed straight from the source, and, according to an enduring myth, is also home to its own hidden monster. Parts of the Vättern, which geologists believe was once connected to the Baltic Sea, feature extensive cliffs dotted with woodland. These cliffsides form a tempting vantage point from which to appreciate the wonders of the lake, with the opposite shore resembling some far-off country. It is an extraordinary place in which to build a house.

Architect Petra Gipp was invited to create a new home here that would make the most of the open panorama of the great lake. 'The dramatic cliffs, the sky and the open water created the conditions for this house,' she says. 'The clients wanted a home in which they could experience the landscape. We had to build a form that followed the terrain, but the site is challenging, with the cliff and the steep drop towards the water, so we created a promenade that follows the contours of the land itself.'

The concrete base and central spine of the house were cast in situ, with the floor level gradually stepping down the cliff face as it slopes towards the edge. A timber envelope of pine was then placed on the pad and to either side of the spine. Outside, the pine appears in its natural state, while inside the timber is painted a soft white, acting as a soothing foil to the exposed concrete surfaces. Accessed from the rear of the house, the central hallway follows the concrete spine, leading through the heart of the building and out towards a cantilevered terrace overlooking the water. To one side of the hallway sit the 'private' areas of the house, with modest bunkrooms complemented by a master bedroom with views of the lake. At the other side is an open-plan living area with a galley kitchen and a seating area, largely consisting of fitted banquettes arranged around a fireplace embedded in the concrete wall, but facing a picture window that frames the open panorama. A shift in floor level, just a few steps, between the kitchen/dining area and the seating zone forms part of an architectural promenade that carries one right through the house.

'The building and nature interact to create a home,' Gipp adds. 'The way that the house is integrated with the outdoors feels particularly Scandinavian. For me, all projects start with a reading of the site to study its layers – historical, as well as topographical. We wanted to occupy the setting with humility and leave nature as untouched as possible.'

The concrete spine at the centre of the house helps define the main circulation route, with bedrooms to one side and living spaces to the other, offering open views of the lake.

The house makes the most of its high vantage point on the cliffs overlooking the expanse of the lake; an elevated terrace supplements the spaces within.

Fleinvær Refugium

Fleinvær, Norway

TYIN Tegnestue,
Rintala Eggertsson

Some years ago, in 2004, musician and composer Håvard Lund bought some land on the small island of Fleinvær, itself part of a distinctive archipelago floating off the northwestern coast of Norway. The remote Arctic setting captured Lund's imagination. 'Fleinvær got to me from the very first moment,' he says. 'Initially, it was meant as a workplace for myself – a writing lodge, of sorts. But as time went on, I felt a need to share what I had found at Fleinvær with others. I wanted to create a workplace unlike anything else in the world.'

Lund's vision was to create a series of residences for visiting artists, writers and musicians – a creative community, or micro-village, in a wild and remote landscape. He turned to two separate architectural practices, TYIN Tegnestue and Rintala Eggertsson, who between them had extensive experience of building in extreme locations and experimenting with contemporary interpretations of cabins, boathouses, treehouses and other vernacular buildings, often expressed in imaginative and sculptural forms. Having surveyed the site with the help of students from the Norwegian University of Science and Technology, the team created a series of modestly scaled and complementary buildings, an approach that has helped to lessen the impact of the community on the land.

'This project was about breaking the programme down into several smaller units, rather than creating one large building,' explains architect Sami Rintala. 'This makes it possible to regulate which units are being warmed, based on the number of visitors, and control the use of energy. The scale of the village and the placing of each unit in the landscape also resonates with the traditional way of building on these islands.'

The community comprises a sequence of micro-cabins that climb the gently sloping shoreline. Closest to the sea sits a sauna placed on an existing dock, with a lodge for overnight guests nearby. As one climbs the hill, there are four cabins, or bunkhouses, which serve as accommodation for the resident artists. Ascending again, one reaches the hub building – a performance space and canteen, with a terrace on the platform between them. Although more communal in nature, this dual building is still modest in scale and height. Clad in durable Kebony timber, the twin structures sit on a platform raised above the surface of the ground by angled steel supports.

The final – and perhaps most extraordinary – building in the sequence sits a little further up the hillside again. This is a 'room of reflection', consisting of an elevated cabin contained within a supporting steel frame and suspended on a single metal pillar. This elevated space offers powerful views of the surrounding islands, and was partly inspired by the *njalla*, a traditional storehouse used by the local Sami people.

The framed view from the 'room of reflection' looks out across the archipelago. The bunkhouses are small but textural, and also offer vistas of the distinctive landscape.

Coastal Retreats   Fleinvær Refugium

The 'room of reflection' forms a floating
watchtower overlooking the rest of the
cabins, including the larger communal
buildings and the smaller bunkhouses.

The collection of buildings forms a modern
micro-community, echoing the traditional
pattern of village living on the islands, with
their clusters of cabins and small houses.

Manshausen Island Resort

Steigen, Norway

Stinessen Arkitektur

Børge Ousland, the Norwegian polar explorer and writer, is, of course, no stranger to extremes when it comes to appreciating the natural world. He made his first solo trip to the North Pole in the mid-1990s, followed by further trips to both poles. As well as writing, film-making and planning expeditions, Ousland has also created an Arctic resort on the small island of Manshausen in northern Norway, between the mountains and the Barents Sea. 'It's really the landscape that plays the main role here,' he says. 'There are very few places on earth where you can find such pristine surroundings, with the sea and the mountains behind a sheltered archipelago of islands, which are accessible yet with very few people.'

Historically, the island was a trading post serving the fishing industry, but few traces of the past remain, apart from an 18th-century farmhouse and a series of stone quays. Having bought the 55-acre island in 2010, Ousland commissioned architect Snorre Stinessen to create a modest resort that could accommodate no more than a few dozen visitors at a time. The original farmhouse was updated, and now offers a dining area and kitchen on the ground floor, as well as a communal library upstairs; an existing cabin from the 1970s has also been updated and an expedition 'loft' added. The most striking structures on the island, however, are the four new cabins designed by Stinessen, with three of these inhabiting the original stone quays and projecting out over the water.

'The quays are the only trace remaining of a fairly large wooden warehouse that once stood on the island, dating back to the time when the waterways were the main communication line along the coast of northern Norway,' the architect explains.

'Utilizing the existing foundation felt right, because it preserves and enhances the history and natural landscape of the island. There would have been room for more cabins, but we chose to give priority to the individual qualities of each one and to emphasize privacy and the individual views.'

The stone quays anchor the timber structures, which float above the sea, rather like berthed boats. Accessed from the rear, they include kitchenettes, a bathroom and a bunkroom, yet the main space hanging over the water is largely open plan and includes a seating area and the master bedroom. Both of these face a wall of floor-to-ceiling glass that forms a kind of maritime observatory; a modest deck alongside offers an outdoor sitting room. The sea cabins are highly contextual in every sense. The decision to create a series of smaller dwellings in a compound formation, rather than a larger hotel building, both reduces the impact of the resort on the island and helps protect the privacy of the families that stay in this escapist Arctic retreat.

Coastal Retreats

Manshausen Island Resort

The cantilevered sleeping cabins frame open views; the portion facing the sea is open plan, holding living and sleeping spaces, with services and the entrance to the rear.

Coastal Retreats

Manshausen Island Resort

'It's really the landscape that plays the main role here. There are very few places on earth where you can find such pristine surroundings, with the sea and the mountains behind a sheltered archipelago of islands, which are accessible yet with very few people.'

Summerhouse Lagnö

Stockholm, Sweden

Tham & Videgård

Within the more extreme environment of the coast, the idea of building a low-maintenance, highly durable home can be a challenge. This was exactly the nature of the brief put to architectural firm Tham & Videgård, whose clients wanted a new summerhouse on one of the many thousands of islands that form the Stockholm archipelago. It needed to be worry-free and able to stand up to the wind and saltwater spray, as well as the particular demands of the Swedish winter.

'The summerhouse is constructed entirely from materials that can withstand the climate here and will age beautifully,' explains architect Bolle Tham. 'Our ambition is always to design functional, beautiful and enduring buildings, and to achieve a resilient architecture. We often say that the oldest house still functioning well is the most sustainable one.'

Given that the island is relatively accessible, the architects were less limited in their choice of construction method than might be the case in more remote corners of the archipelago. Ultimately, they decided to use precast concrete, which is not only weather-resistant and requires little upkeep, but also echoes visually the granite bedrock of the site. Cast in situ, the concrete lends the house a degree of sculptural monumentality, mitigated by the relatively low height of the largely single-storey building and softened by the backdrop of woodland behind it.

The house also plays with vernacular references and forms in a contemporary manner, and comprises a series of interconnected pitched-roof volumes, which the architects compare to a line of boathouses, with the gables creating a 'pleated long façade'. Three pitched roofs of varying proportions float above the main portion of the house, while a fourth protects the guest house, which sits on the same axis. Between the two buildings, a fifth roof of steel and glass floats above an open-ended veranda, separating the enclosed portions of the summerhouse and doubling as a sheltered entrance zone.

'The gable roofs provide a sequence of varied interior heights and create zones in an otherwise completely open main room, stretching the entire length of the building,' says architect Martin Videgård. 'With a relatively shallow room depth and a continuous, sliding-glass partition out to the terrace, the space acts as a niche in relation to the archipelago landscape outside.'

This open living space, with areas for seating and dining, frames the vista of the water, taking advantage of its relatively elevated position on the site. Sliding timber doors to the rear of the multifunctional living room protect the sequence of modestly scaled bedrooms, and the kitchen and bathroom at the rear of the building. The independent guest house nearby features a similar spatial arrangement, while allowing visiting friends and family a degree of privacy. With a swimming pool alongside the house and a sauna down the hill, a little closer to the shore, the arrangement creates a summer compound that meets the ambitions of both architect and client with success.

In both the main building and the guest house the living spaces are positioned to the front, facing the views, with kitchenettes, services and bedrooms to the rear. The guest house also features a sleeping loft.

Coastal Retreats   Summerhouse Lagnö

The sawtooth roofline lends character and helps lessen the impact of the house. The gap between the main building and the guest house serves as an outdoor room, partially protected by the steel-and-glass canopy.

Townhouses

In some respects, the towns and cities of the Nordic countries face the same problems as any other urban centre. The car continues to rule and there are mounting pressures around traffic management versus pedestrianization and pollution control. Then there are the familiar arguments regarding affordability and urban density, along with ongoing debates about increasing urban sprawl versus rising building heights, which clearly impact upon the skyline while providing more living space in high-demand areas.

In others, however, Scandinavia is blessed many times over. Cities such as Copenhagen, Stockholm, Oslo, Helsinki, Gothenburg and Bergen are scenic and seldom feel overcrowded, in comparison with other European urban centres. Nordic towns and cities also tend to be less constrained in terms of space for expansion and evolution, with significant progress in reclaiming former industrial zones for fresh construction and development. Many are located along the coast, focused around trade and sea routes, which lends them a sense of openness. Connection with the water tends to mitigate pollution, as well, giving these settings a degree of freshness and vitality.

A number of the houses in this chapter – including Elding Oscarson's Mölle by the Sea (p. 178) and Villa R (p. 202) by Arkitekterna Krook & Tjäder, both in Sweden – have suburban contexts, but also offer vivid connections with the sea. Green and leafy settings also allow for the possibility of significant indoor–outdoor relationships. A key example is Villa S (p. 190) by Saunders Architecture in Bergen, Norway, which sits within a leftover plot in a garden city laid out in the 1930s. Surrounded by trees and greenery, the design of this family home partly revolves around the creation of outdoor rooms and fresh-air spaces, as well as elevated rooms within that serve as belvederes looking out over the grounds.

Within such surroundings, a familiar emphasis on organic materials comes into play, comparable with the more rural examples of the contemporary Nordic home. Villa S features timber cladding stained black, while Villa R is coated in strips of cedar, and so on. A family home in Aarhus, Denmark (p. 184), designed by Martin and Mette Wienberg in collaboration with architectural firm Friis & Moltke, features pine cladding, also stained black, and key living spaces inside that are panelled with oak, lending the house a highly crafted quality. Like a number of other houses featured here, there is no sense of imaginative constraint suggested by the limitations of the urban environment. The house has a dynamic and sculptural quality that is also seen in other projects.

For architect Sigurd Larsen's Roof House (p. 196) in Copenhagen, the relatively small suburban site and equally modest budget were no great impediments to the design of an innovative, experimental home, in which the 'fifth façade' – the roof – becomes a key part of the identity and spatial integrity of the building. As with many of the houses in this chapter, the manipulation and management of natural light was a key concern, balanced with the need for privacy. 'Although Nordic sunlight is very particular in its cold, blue tone and texture, it is, of course, scarce, especially in winter,' Larsen explains. 'Light was at the forefront of our scheme, so I think that you can think of the Roof House as Scandinavian, while the abundant use of wood as the main construction material is rooted in Danish design.'

Even in tighter streetscapes, imaginative responses are possible, also involving a particular emphasis on natural light and creating a sense of volumetric openness. In this respect, Elding Oscarson's Townhouse (p. 172) in the Swedish coastal town of Landskrona is a prime example. Although hemmed in by neighbouring buildings, the house manages to feel both light and open through a combination of spatial dexterity, using double-height spaces within the floorplan, as well as connections to a hidden courtyard garden to the rear and a secret roof terrace on the uppermost floor. In such ways, an urban Nordic home becomes a place of welcome and architectural innovation.

Villa Björnberget

Nacka, Sweden

Delin Arkitektkontor

The design and build of Villa Björnberget was undertaken in two stages. Situated in a leafy, suburban district of Stockholm, the project began with an outwardly simple design by architect Buster Delin that took inspiration from the shape and form of vernacular barns and farm buildings. Built with a relatively modest budget, the original house featured a framework of glulam timber beams, spruce cladding and a zinc roof, while inside, a central kitchen and dining area occupied a partially double-height space. To one side was a seating area; to the other, a separate master suite, complete with bathroom and sauna. Additional space was contained in a loft upstairs, which crossed the central void via a lacquered steel bridge.

With its concrete floor, exposed timber ceilings and extensive glazing, the house had a pleasing character of its own, but just four years later, the clients came back with a request for an extension that would hold a new family room, plus extra loft space, as well as semi-separate guest accommodation that could be rented out. This new extension needed to complement the existing building, rather than undermine it, as well as the garden. Delin came up with a solution that has given fresh life and character to the house, enhancing its functional and spatial aspects, and creating a more accomplished composition.

The two parts of the new brief are contained in a pair of distinctive structures, each with its own pitched roof, in the same materials as the master barn. This triptych of buildings has been staggered on the site, connected only at the corners, a stepped formation that gave the architect the opportunity to create a series of terraces at either side of the freshly extended home, offering a choice of private or more 'public' outdoor rooms.

'Villa Björnberget is both a simple, easy-to-read house, and a complex structure that provides unexpected spaces, views and private hideaways,' Delin says. 'I'm fond of the graphic expression of the roofline in contrast to the softness of the sky.'

At the same time, the house suggests that architectural innovation can be achieved on a relatively modest scale and in suburban settings. Splitting the evolution of the house into two parts has clearly helped to make the project more affordable, and has also resulted in a home that is more than the sum of its parts.

'I often work with clients who are very conscious of architecture and design, but don't have large budgets,' adds the architect. 'This has led to a good understanding of how to use materials and construct interesting houses with less money. The focus is always on how the house is experienced as you move in and out, how light and materials interact, and how the house incorporates the natural world around it.'

Townhouses   Villa Björnberget

The ground floor is dominated by a black-and-white colour scheme, while the loft spaces in the old and new parts of the house feature bare blond timber on the floors or ceilings.

Townhouses

Villa Björnberget

'I often work with clients who are very conscious about architecture and design, but don't have large budgets. This has led to a good understanding of how to use materials and construct interesting houses with less money.'

In the original part of the house, a steel bridge spans the double-height living space and connects the loft spaces at either end. The design accentuates the sense of height and volume in this part of the building, which is reminiscent of a barn.

Townhouse

Landskrona, Sweden

Elding Oscarson

The crisp, white façade of Johnny Lökaas and Conny Ahlgren's home stands out among the eclectic mix of houses on their street in the Swedish town of Landskrona. The buildings here, close to the centre of the town, are a melange of size, scales and periods, with this new design by architects Elding Oscarson being the latest addition. The design is uncompromising in its sense of modernity, owing little to vernacular Scandinavian traditions, yet is also a very specific response to the challenges of the site and the particular brief provided by the clients, an interior designer and café owner/art dealer.

Landskrona sits on the coast between Helsingborg to the north and Malmö to the south. For much of the 20th century, it was home to a large shipyard and had a ferry service to Copenhagen, located on the opposite shore of the Øresund strait (now it is simpler to drive to Malmö via the road bridge, which opened in 2000). The couple acquired two houses in the town in 2005, and some years later began to think about creating a new home in the long back garden of one of them, which had a gap in the parallel streetscape where a house had been demolished in the 1940s. 'The site is barely 5 m (16 ft) wide and faces a picturesque street, as well as a courtyard,' says architect Jonas Elding. 'The historic setting is of key importance, and the house contributes by creating a contrast that works as an eye-opener for the beauty, colour and diversity of its context.'

Elding's clients prepared a detailed wish list for the project. 'We wanted a lot of space for our art collection, but also a lot of light, as well as some office space, a garden and some privacy from the traffic,' they explain.

Meeting the brief within the constraints of the site required an imaginative response. Using masonry blocks finished with an exterior render, the architects created a three-storey home that is relatively closed around the main entrance, where the building connects to the street, but opens up to the rear and as it ascends. At ground-floor level, it features a largely open-plan kitchen and dining area, feeding out at the back to a sheltered courtyard garden; beyond this is a small, single-storey pavilion with a green roof, which provides office space. Staggered double-height spaces within the main house, as one climbs to the upper two levels, enhance both the sense of space and natural light. A welcoming sitting room/library is positioned at mid-level, while the master suite and a semi-enclosed roof terrace inhabit the upper storey. The house was also designed to be highly energy-efficient.

'We like the location on this quiet street in the middle of the town, as well as the openness, light and modernity of the house,' Lökaas explains. 'I have come to realize that you don't really need that much space to live in, but the smaller the house is, the more good qualities – light, openness and warmth – you need.'

Townhouses   Townhouse

The main living space is at the mid-level of the house and features a window seat looking out across the streetscape. The ground-floor kitchen/dining room flows out to a hidden courtyard garden, with a single-storey pavilion beyond holding a dedicated office.

Townhouses

Townhouse

The staggered formation of the main building allows for significant shifts in height and volume. The uppermost level features an integrated roof terrace at the front and a bedroom to the rear, connected by a bridge spanning the spaces below.

Townhouses   Townhouse

Mölle by the Sea

Mölle, Sweden

Elding Oscarson

In the 19th century Mölle, situated at the end of the Kulla peninsula and overlooking the mouth of the Øresund strait, was a thriving fishing village, complete with its own harbour and lighthouse nearby. Towards the end of the century, the village reinvented itself as a holiday resort, helped by a tolerant attitude to mixed-sex bathing, which was still unusual at the time. Visitors began arriving from across Europe, and from Germany in particular, with hotels and holiday homes adopting a mix of architectural styles from around the world.

Architects Jonas Elding and Johan Oscarson embraced this spirit of semi-bohemian diversity in their design for a new and distinctly modern holiday home, situated upon a hillside setting within the town. Elding had spent time in Tokyo working with the Japanese practice SANAA, and Oscarson had worked in Stockholm with architect and designer Thomas Sandell; collectively, their work draws inspiration from many quarters, with a focus on innovative structural and spatial solutions.

'Our design tries to sidestep generic Scandinavian design, and follows Mölle's tradition of affluent, non-Scandinavian architecture,' explains Elding. 'Some materials and methods, however – the careful use of wood, for example – could be interpreted as Scandinavian, although it is actually a reference to some of the Alpine-style log houses in the neighbourhood.'

The clients commissioned a family home for use at weekends and holidays. The sloping site looks out across neighbouring houses to the sea and along the coastline, with an old ice cellar in the garden, bordered by stone and brick walls. The new building sits on a grassy plateau within a Y-shaped plan, with the splayed wings facing the open vista. A largely transparent lower level holds most of the principal living spaces in an open-plan formation arranged around two service pods. Slender steel piloti support the rest of the house, allowing for walls of glass at ground level. The floor above, which holds three bedrooms and a family room, is more enclosed and clad in broad boards of Douglas fir. The oversized plans accentuate the mass of this part of the house, which seems to float above the rest, while playing with conventional attitudes to timber cabins. A basement level holds a guest bedroom and service spaces.

'We wanted to create a semi-outdoor living space,' Elding adds. 'It feels like being in a garden, or in an orangery, even though you are still inside. Yet it is also functional and inhabitable in a vivid and relaxed way.'

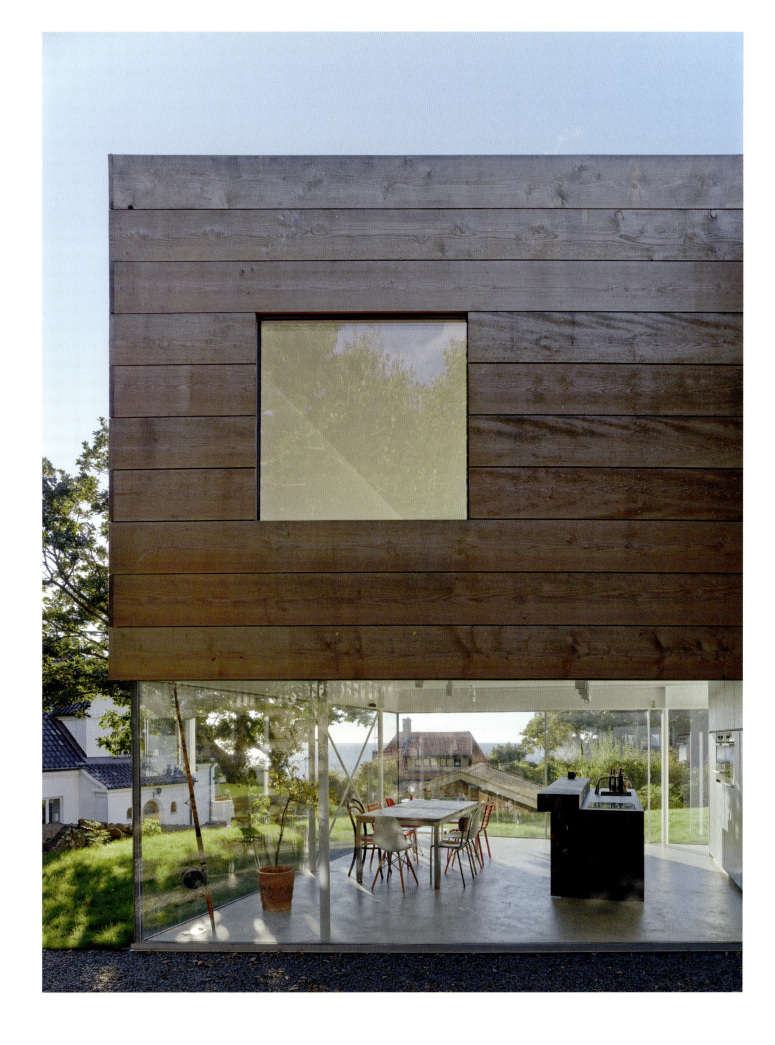

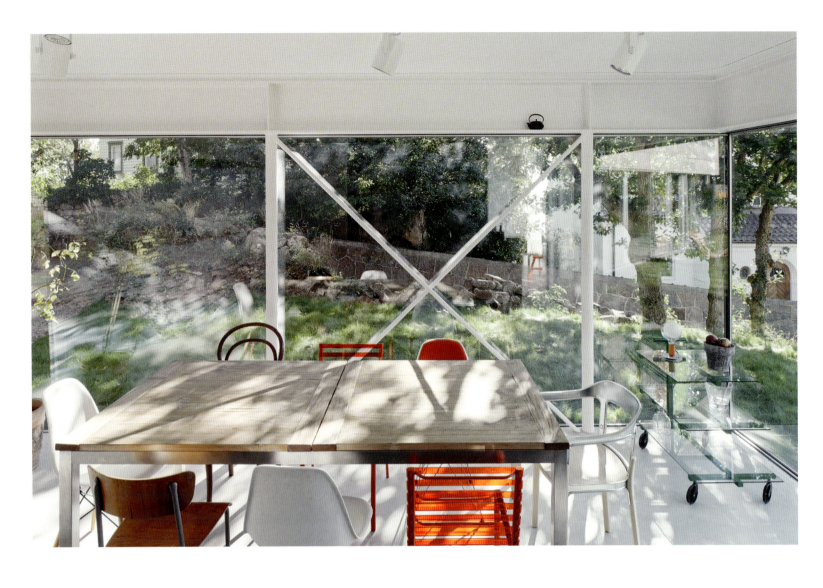

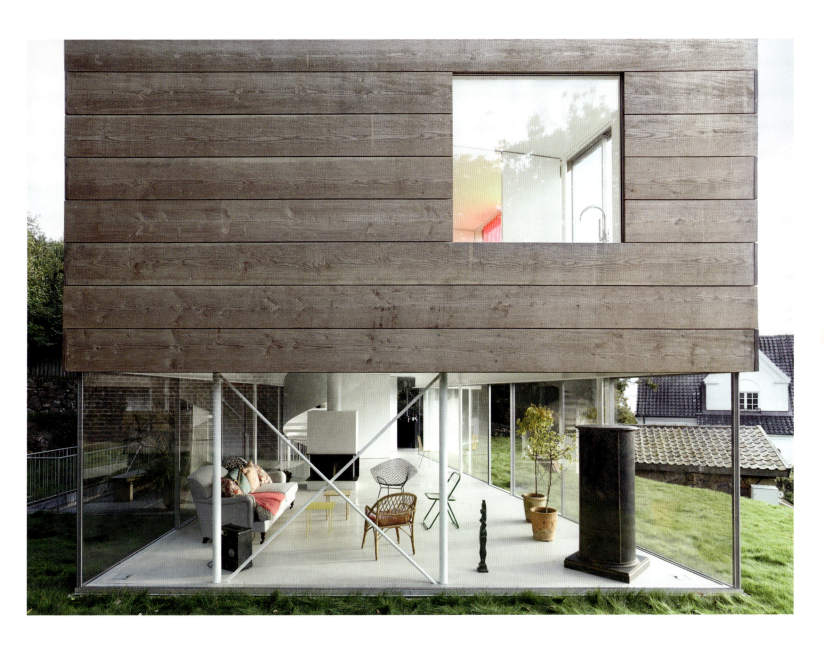

The design establishes a vibrant contrast
between mass and transparency, with the
more enclosed, timber-clad upper storey
floating above the glazed walls of the main
living space below.

The house uses its elevated, hillside position to best advantage, opening up to the views across the town and towards the coast, while adopting a trefoil formation.

Villa Wienberg

Aarhus, Denmark

Wienberg Architecs &
Friis & Moltke Architects

Aarhus, located on the eastern coast of the Jutland peninsula and the 2017 European Capital of Culture, is the second-largest city in Denmark, as well as its fastest growing, swallowing up neighbouring towns and villages – including Højbjerg, which lies to the south, where architects Mette and Martin Wienberg came across a small summer cottage. Dating from the 1940s, the house sits within a leafy corner site, bordered by pine trees and rhododendrons. This verdant setting captured the couple's imagination and spurred the design of a new family home, which has engulfed the old cottage.

'It is the forest character of the surroundings that makes the location so special,' says Martin Wienberg. 'We wanted to take advantage of these qualities and create spaces that enhance our daily lives, which are both comfortable and inspirational. The theme was adaptation to our surroundings, but we were also very inspired by buildings we have seen in Japan and in Finland.'

Enlisting the assistance of architectural firm Friis & Moltke, the Wienbergs came up with a new design that makes the most of this green suburban enclave. From the outside, the house, which is shared with the couple's son Oscar, is dominated by a two-storey tower, with a single-storey structure alongside. Both elements are clad in black-stained pine, lending the composition a distinctive abstract quality. Large picture windows pierce the façade and connect with the garden. Inside, the interplay between the two parts creates a startling dynamic with a series of contrasts between the open spaces and more intimate retreats, complemented by shifts in materiality, texture and colour. From the porched entrance, the interiors reveal themselves gradually, offering a series of engaging surprises.

Most striking of all are the two spaces contained in the front section of the 'tower', overlooking the grounds. On the ground floor sits an oak-panelled family room, which combines many functions, as well as connecting with most of the key spaces in the house in one way or another. The room is bordered by fitted benches, which provide seating around the window views. To one side is a library wall and a crafted staircase leading up to a study, also timber-panelled, which can be seen as a complementary extension of the space below. This crafted space is reminiscent of the 'soft modernism' of Finnish master architects like Alvar Aalto.

At the same time, the house explores connections between indoors and out in a number of ways. While the large picture windows frame views of the garden, a hidden courtyard at the centre of the house doubles as a lightwell. This helps to bring natural light – and a sense of the world outside – into the master bedroom, while additional living spaces sit to the rear of the plan. Fitted storage throughout helps maintain a visual purity within this suburban forest home.

Townhouses

Villa Wienberg

The family room is a highly crafted space, with oak panelling and fitted elements such as seating and bookcases. The courtyard doubles as a lightwell and outdoor room.

Townhouses   Villa Wienberg

The timber-clad tower, with the main living space on the ground floor and a study above, dominates the site. There is also a roof terrace alongside, which forms one of a range of outdoor living spaces.

188

Townhouses   Villa Wienberg

Villa S

Bergen, Norway

Saunders Architecture

During the 1930s, the pioneering modernist architect Leif Grung planned 'Tveiterås', a new garden city on former farmland at the southern edge of the Norwegian town of Bergen. New houses were largely made out of timber and carefully arranged within the landscape. Over the years, as the trees and vegetation have matured, this 'garden city' has lived up to its name. Canadian-born architect Todd Saunders, who first settled in Norway in the 1990s, was drawn to a rare and vacant plot of land within Tveiterås, and it was here that he decided to build a home for himself and his family.

The site was overgrown, but Saunders immediately saw the potential for creating a building that would connect with nature, even in this suburban context. This 21st-century version of a timber-clad home has a horizontal band of living space cantilevered from a supporting tower, a floating platform for daily living that both offers a treehouse-style sense of connection with the restored gardens and, importantly, provides shelter for the all-weather veranda below.

'The design was partly a reaction to the weather,' he says. 'It rains a lot here, so I lifted the house up to create a covered area, which means that the building protects you from the elements, even when you are outside. It was a negative reaction, but with a positive result. My children can play underneath the house and we can sit outside, even when it is pouring with rain.'

Clad in spruce, stained black, the framework of the house is made from steel and timber. The ground level of the tower features a television den, alongside the entrance hall and stairway, which climbs up to the main body of the building. Here, an elevated

kitchen/dining area sits at the heart of the platform. The children's bedrooms and a sitting room are at one end of the house, with the master bedroom suite at the other. There are also two balconies, one of them connecting to the roof of a storage pod below, which doubles as an additional support for the house and triples as a secondary access via a hidden staircase. The upper level holds a spacious library, leading out onto a substantial roof deck; here, looking out, one is literally among the treetops. The interior treatment in the library, as elsewhere, is light and soothing, with white ceilings and walls, and exposed Dinesen timber floors. The open and airy character of the interiors contrasts with the dark materiality of the exterior. One's eye is constantly drawn outside, connecting with the trees and the garden city.

'The house is very comfortable and works really well for us,' Saunders says. 'It's like a well-oiled engine and reflects my own aesthetic, with all of these natural, high-quality materials. Also, it ages extremely well.'

Townhouses   Villa S

The main living spaces are all situated on the piano nobile, overlooking the gardens below. The staircase here ascends to a library, positioned on the modest upper level.

The design offers a series of outdoor rooms suited to all kinds of weather, including a sheltered play area beneath the house and integrated decks at mid-level.

Roof House

Copenhagen, Denmark

Sigurd Larsen

Danish architect Sigurd Larsen talks about the growing importance of the 'fifth façade' – the rooflines of houses and buildings, which have been assuming significance and visibility as urban environments become increasingly built up and elevated. This fifth façade was a key part of the design approach for Roof House in Copenhagen, in which the roof assumes a dynamic, sculptural form. The context of the project is actually gentle suburbia, with the house surrounded by low-slung, timber-clad neighbours. Yet in this setting, too, the irregular and energetic roofline of the single-storey house is particularly visible, given the gently pitching roofs of the neighbouring buildings.

'The site is in a residential area of Copenhagen, surrounded by typical single-family homes,' explains Larsen, who worked with Rem Koolhaas at OMA and at MVRDV, before founding his own practice. 'Our project aimed to set itself apart from the rest, while following the same zoning plan. With its complex roof structure, the design plays with the special Scandinavian light, while maintaining a Nordic feel through its use of materials.'

The new house sits on a relatively modest corner plot, bordered by access lanes and neighbours. Maintaining privacy for the clients – a family with two children – while maximizing the potential of the site was a key challenge in itself. This was achieved not only by the careful orientation of the new building and the thoughtful placement of windows, but also through the creation of two semi-enclosed courtyards, or verandas, within the overall outline of the building. These twin courtyards create more intimate and sheltered outdoor rooms, and act as a partial screen for banks of glazing that connect with the key internal living spaces.

With the exception of the courtyards and an entrance at the opposite side of the building, the rest of the larch-clad house is protected by a complex roofscape of intersecting diagonals, punctuated by skylights. Externally, the roofline required careful planning, not just in terms of geometrical composition, but also in managing rainwater. Internally, the shifting ceilings, clad in pine, play an important role in subtly differentiating zones within the mostly open-plan living space, helping to define the seating area from the kitchen/diner. Walls are in a crisp white and the floors are polished concrete, helping in the circulation of natural light. Bedrooms and bathrooms are arranged around the entrance zone at the other end of the building.

'The key requirement from our clients was to design a house that felt spacious and bright, despite the small footprint,' Larsen says. 'In terms of privacy, they wanted something that felt private, while staying away from the typical high garden hedges that are often used – and hated – in Danish suburbs. The response to this was to create courtyards around the house, which act like a buffer between inside and out. But the main idea was to use the roofscape as a filter for daylight, allowing different tones of light and colour to enter various parts of the house throughout the day.'

Townhouses   Roof House

The shifting roofline helps to define different zones within the fluid, open-plan living space. Even in this urban context, the design ensures privacy and connectivity with the outdoors.

Townhouses   Roof House

A series of terraces and sheltered courtyards offer a choice of outdoor rooms, while also serving as a buffer between the house and the city beyond.

Townhouses   Roof House

Villa R

Ljungskile, Sweden

Arkitekterna Krook & Tjäder

There is an argument that suggests that the most sustainable kind of home is a flexible one. Rather than confining its inhabitants to a set pattern of living, the flexible home adapts with ease to changing family circumstances over time, or the arrival of extended family or friends. This is very much the case with Villa R, located in the Swedish coastal town of Ljungskile, north of Gothenburg. Designed by architectural firm Krook & Tjäder, the house can make significant claims towards sustainability in a number of respects.

'The area is located where the archipelago meets the forest of the mainland, and the site itself is a former boatyard that was heavily contaminated,' says architect Christian Hammarström. 'Extensive decontamination was required on site and along the old quayside. The clients wanted to live in a "barefoot" house, with room for their grown-up children and visiting friends and family. The design is tailor-made and calm, with an intimate scale in terms of the details, but also with the potential to host a bustling party.'

This compound home by the water comprises a number of related elements. A low-slung pavilion at the entrance serves as a spacious but separate four-bedroomed guest house, which can be closed down or opened back up again, according to need. A series of service and storage spaces is contained in another pavilion, which leads down to a dock at the water's edge. The main house opens out onto a terrace, orientated towards the sea. With the exception of an elevated family room on an upper level, the living spaces and the master suite are located on the ground floor, which includes a double-height atrium and glass-encased indoor garden. This hidden solarium doubles as a lightwell, introducing an uplifting element at the heart of the house.

The key living spaces revolve around the atrium and the solarium, as well as connecting with the terrace. The master suite sits within a sequence of spaces to one side of the main building, including a sauna and plunge-pool, faced in timber and suggesting Japanese, as well as Scandinavian, influences. The entire house, including the pavilions, has been clad in slats of cedar over a steel framework, while oak was used for much of the internal joinery. The flat roofs are coated in sedum and the main energy source is geothermal. For much of the time, the owners use only the main house, reducing overall energy consumption.

'The house has a certain air of modesty and control,' Hammarström adds. 'But it also responds to and takes in the natural world around it.'

Townhouses

Villa R

Double-height living spaces and a hidden courtyard garden introduce light and character to the main part of the house, which also makes use of textural materials.

Townhouses   Villa R

The interiors frame key vistas of the coast, while the landscaping offers a series of terraces and courtyards. The use of cedar slats across the compound helps to tie the elements together within a clear vocabulary.

Townhouses

Villa R

Villa Kristina

Gothenburg, Sweden

Wingårdh Arkitektkontor

Sitting at the suburban edge of Sweden's second city is a parcel of land that has been in Kristina Lagercrantz's family for generations. In the early 1900s the area was mostly farmland, and the family built a summerhouse here. Her grandmother still lives next door in a house built in the 1980s, by which time Gothenburg's expanding suburbs had swallowed up the farms and provided new neighbours. Capturing the atmosphere of a rural villa, while maintaining a sense of privacy, offered a key challenge in the design of a new family home for Lagercrantz and her family.

'We wanted a "secret" getaway and a grand feeling in a small house,' her husband Anders Bergström explains. 'But we also wanted to use local materials and to create exciting, surprising architecture that wasn't too expensive. We wanted to blend into the environment, without blasting away rocks or tearing down trees.'

The couple had long admired the villa designs of architect Gert Wingårdh, and a friend of the family who worked at Wingårdh's Gothenburg-based firm believed that the challenges facing their build might be of interest to him. The practice designed a courtyard house that floats above the ground on a series of concrete pillars to cause minimal disturbance to the site. It turns its largely closed back on the neighbours and access road. The majority of the house is, indeed, 'secret', revealing itself gradually as one steps through the closed, enigmatic façade of whitewashed spruce.

Bedrooms, bathrooms and service spaces all sit within a private wing of the U-shaped home. The rest of the building has a sequence of more open, dynamic living spaces, including a substantial kitchen and dining area at the centre of the floorplan, with a long dining table that can seat 16. Beyond is the lounge and a music space, with a study contained within the upper level of a tower above. From here, the views lead out across the landscape and towards the coastline in the distance. Banks of glazing connect the ground-floor living spaces to the courtyard, which forms a semi-sheltered outdoor room. A processional staircase leads up to a roof deck, an arrangement somewhat reminiscent of Le Corbusier's roof terrace at Villa Savoye, outside Paris. Another point of reference for the design was Alvar Aalto's Experimental House in Finland, which is also arranged around a hidden courtyard.

'We like the calmness of the house, as well as the sense of surprise when you enter from the outside,' Bergström continues. 'All of the materials were produced in southern Sweden, and the plants, flowers and trees in the garden are all native to the area. We didn't want the "luxury" of imports like Italian marble, but for everything to be of high quality and locally produced.'

Townhouses   Villa Kristina

The living spaces are arranged around the central courtyard, which provides a hidden garden, as well as light and air. The outdoor staircase ascends to the roof terrace.

The tower contains a study with a view on the upper level, floating above a music room below. The house's largely closed façade is orientated towards the street and neighbours.

Country Homes

The vernacular architecture of rural Scandinavia still forms a vivid point of inspiration for architects working today. There is a highly appealing quality to the mountain cabins, fishermen's cottages and farmsteads of the Nordic countries, and the natural modesty of these traditional buildings, their organic materiality and the way they sit within the landscape make them an influential source of reference – rather more so, perhaps, than the grander country houses and estates of the region. Such typologies influenced the Nordic masters of the modernist period – Alvar Aalto, Bruno Mathsson, Sverre Fehn – and were woven into new ways of working and fresh approaches to space, volume and the integration of indoor and outdoor living spaces. Such homes continue to play a crucial part in the cultural make-up of Scandinavia.

Along with the rural cabin (see chapter 1), one of the most powerful and traditional ideals in Nordic design and architecture is that of the farmstead. The barn, with its engaging simplicity of form, has a cultural importance that goes far beyond its original purpose. Built with local materials, this simple building seems to both emerge from the landscape and shelter within it. Many architects tell stories of childhood experiences of visiting barns and being overwhelmed by the sheer scale and impressive openness. Farmhouses, too, have that sense of the organic, being deeply rooted in a place, partly born of function, but also shaped by the availability of materials and the skills of craftsmen and artisans. The spaces of a farmhouse have modesty, as well as texture and warmth, with the idea of the hearth forming an essential component.

More than this, the farmstead has a collective power that comes from a combination of home, barns, stables and agricultural sheds and outhouses. Often, this collection of structures will be arranged around a farmyard or central court, helping to protect and encircle this partially enclosed outdoor space. The synergy of such assemblies and the way that a number of modestly scaled buildings sit together has helped to shape the evolution of contemporary houses and villas that are a sum of their parts. These 'compound' houses offer a series of complementary structures suited to different functions and purposes. A main residence might sit alongside a guest pavilion, or an atelier, or perhaps a separate sauna, within a modest assembly. Offering a series of smaller structures, rather than one larger house, helps to reduce the impact of the villa on its surroundings, while helping to frame outdoor rooms, decks and terraces that themselves help to dissolve boundaries between inside and outside space.

A number of homes in this book were conceived within the ambition of creating a 21st-century farmstead. This is particularly true of Slutterupgård (p. 246) in Denmark, by Henning Larsen, which provides not just a home for its owners, but also stables for a stud farm and other farm buildings within one cohesive programme bound by a common architectural approach. C. F. Møller's Villa G (p. 234), also in Denmark, and OOPEAA's House Riihi (p. 256) in Finland similarly reference vernacular farmsteads in a conscious, considered way, creating small collections of interrelated, single-storey structures arranged around a central court.

Other villas draw upon different strands of the vernacular, including colour palettes, materials and craft techniques. Architects Bornstein Lyckefors, for instance, use falu red, a colour traditionally associated with farmhouses, for the timber cladding of House for a Drummer (p. 222) in Sweden, and yet the form of the house and the spaces inside it are highly contemporary. For Villa Blåbär (p. 262), PS Arkitektur used variants of the black façades and claddings seen on barns and fishermen's huts across the Nordic countries, while Jonas Lindvall's Villa N1 (p. 268) marries traditional forms, such as barn-style structures or timber-clad pavilions, with a more experimental approach to space, volume and contrasts between the communal and private areas of a home.

Such homes reinforce the importance of context within Nordic residential architecture, particularly in more rural areas, yet the significance of context expresses itself in other important ways as well, with architecture that responds to very specific sites and settings. A vital aspect of the Nordic villa is the way in which it connects to the landscape and forms a dynamic sense of connection with the surroundings. In some instances, where the setting has a unique and mesmerizing quality, the wish to respond to the view itself becomes a key driver for the design of the house.

In some projects, spaces become focused like lenses upon different vistas, leading to a more complex form and plan for the building as a whole. This was very much the case with the design of Reiulf Ramstad's Split View Mountain Lodge (p. 274) in Norway, where parts of the main living spaces fork and divide to help frame twin vistas of the mountains. Similar considerations inform the design of Four Cornered Villa (p. 216) by Avanto Architects, in Finland, and Hans Murman's Villa Sunnanö (p. 240) in Sweden, which is split into multiple strands to capture a range of views of the lake. This thoughtful emphasis on contexts, both physical and cultural, helps to enrich modern Nordic architecture and set it apart in the world.

Four Cornered Villa

Virrat, Finland

Avanto Architects

One of the greatest wonders of the Scandinavian countries is the extraordinary natural beauty of the landscape. The lakes, mountains and forests are an intrinsic part of the character and culture of the region, yet also serve as an essential habitat for flora, fauna and wildlife of all kinds. Within this context, sustainability has – naturally – become a key concern for Nordic architects and designers, who feel the responsibility of building in the landscape very keenly. For the design of Four Cornered Villa, architects Ville Hara and Anu Puustinen sought to create a home that was off the grid, while making as little impact on its surroundings as possible.

'The basic idea was to provide an example of a sustainable cottage that would serve as a contrast to other Finnish cottages, which are heated year round to prevent the pipes from freezing,' explains Hara, who was also, along with his family, the client for the project. 'The house is well insulated and heated by wood from our own forest, resulting in a carbon-neutral building.'

Four Cornered Villa is situated in the municipality of Virrat, a largely rural area around three hours' drive north of Helsinki. The site sits on a small, horseshoe-shaped island in Lake Vaskivesi, one of the larger lakes that punctuate the countryside, and was formerly occupied by a modest hut built in the 1960s to house construction workers who were building a new road. Later, the hut was dragged across the frozen lake bed to the island. Hara spent two years studying the site before developing a cruciform, single-storey timber home, with the four spurs of the plan facing different views via a series of floor-to-ceiling windows; two semi-sheltered verandas, or porches, are also contained within the outline of the building.

Outside, the timber cladding has been stained black, while within the floors and panelling have been oiled and stained in a very light finish, creating a vivid contrast between the bright interiors and the subtle exterior, which blends into the ranks of the nearby tree trunks. The main living spaces are open plan, with a subtle sense of separation for the one bedroom in the house. Two wood-burning stoves provide heat for the super-insulated building, assisted by solar gain, while solar panels harness the sun's energy for electricity. A sauna is contained within a separate building, closer to the lake, and here, too, the heating comes from a wood-burning stove, while water is collected on site.

Built with a modest budget and using sustainably sourced timber, the house is an exemplar of a low-carbon approach to the design and build of rural homes. 'Vegetables and herbs are grown on site and the lake is known as a good place to catch pike and perch,' says Hara. 'The simple and ascetic life in the countryside here is dramatically different from more hectic city life, and provides the opportunity to have a minimum impact on nature.'

Country Homes

Four Cornered Villa

The free-flowing interiors of the cruciform plan are crafted and light, while picture windows frame views of the forest. Wood-burning stoves, fuelled by local timber, are the key source of heat.

'The basic idea was to provide an example of a sustainable cottage that would serve as a contrast to typical Finnish cottages, which are heated year round to prevent the pipes from freezing. The house is well insulated and heated by wood from our own forest, resulting in a carbon-neutral building.'

House for a Drummer

Kärna, Sweden

Bornstein Lyckefors Architects

Falu red, commonly painted on the outside of farmhouses and barns, is a traditional favourite in Sweden and other parts of Scandinavia. The name comes from the copper mine at Falun, where some of the mineral ingredients for the pigment originally came from; these were then blended with rye flour, linseed oil and water. During the 17th century, falu red was used on timber houses as it suggested the colour of brick, and became popular again with farmers two centuries later.

Architects Per Bornstein and Andreas Lyckefors were drawn to the colour for the exterior of their rural house, north of Gothenburg, which draws some inspiration from agricultural warehouses and barns, within a decidedly contemporary form. House for a Drummer was commissioned by a single father with two young children and a passion for music. It sits in an area of open farmland and woods, around 30 minutes' drive from the city and not far from the coast; the salt air carries inland on the breeze. A warehouse and roadside store formerly stood on the site, but burned down around the turn of the 19th century. Curiously, it transpires that Lyckefors's own great-great-grandfather used to run the shop.

'This discovery made us revise the design,' Bornstein explains. 'The new house is now a warehouse-inspired volume with distinct framing, and large barnyard doors covering the west-facing windows. The greatest challenge, however, was to create a small house that felt big and to explore the house in three dimensions.'

From the outside, the house has a pleasing sense of scale and geometry, with the red façade standing out against the backdrop of the woodland behind. Yet the box-like form has been subtly subverted on each façade, with irregular windows, apertures and openings, and an integrated balcony around an inset window, making the simple symmetry of the house more complex. Inside, the complexity becomes even more apparent. At ground-floor level, the house is dominated by an open-plan living space with a double-height ceiling and vast sliding windows, protected as needed by barn-door shutters. A dining area and kitchen sit alongside, while service spaces are pushed to the back of the house.

As one ascends upwards, the volumetric exploration of a vertical, as well as horizontal, space becomes apparent, with the upper two storeys stepped and staggered and revolving around the 'great hall' on the ground floor below. A family den and children's bedrooms are positioned at mid-floor level, while the master suite is on the uppermost floor. 'The interior is a continuous flow of space,' Bornstein adds. 'It is rewarding to see how well the house works for the family and how it frames everyday life, but also how the surrounding landscape becomes one with the building.'

The simplicity of the cubic form is playfully undermined inside and out. Interiors step gradually upwards from the ground-floor living spaces to create a series of shifting volumes and galleries.

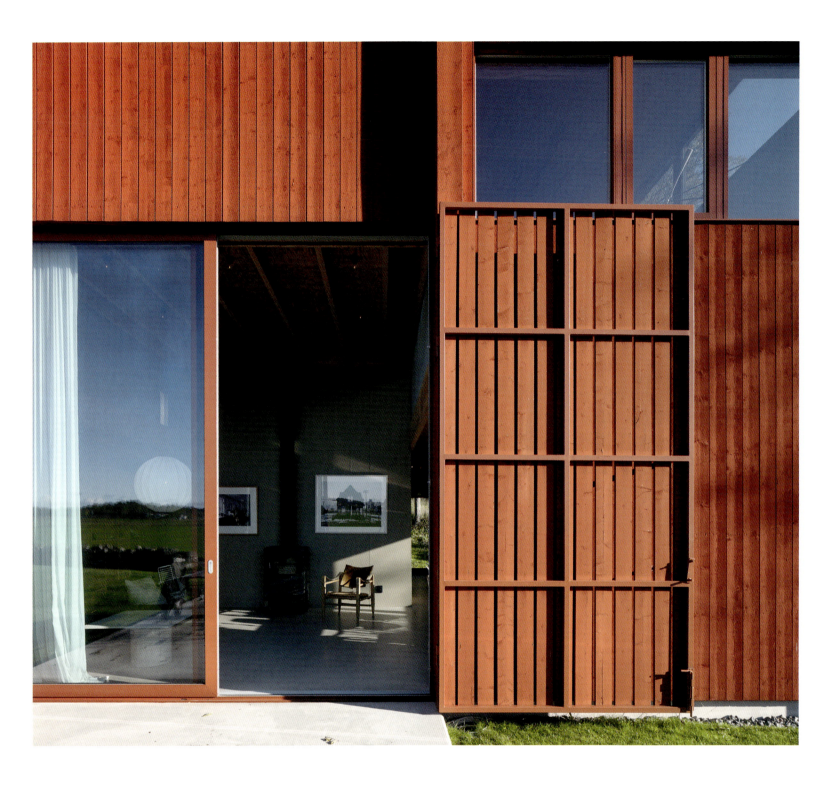

Large, sliding barn-style doors help to protect the windows and reference the traditional use of falu red for the timber. The composition of the fenestration, however, remains distinctly modern.

Plus House

Vendelsö, Sweden

Claesson Koivisto Rune

There are many 'pluses' to the design and build of a prefabricated home, which generally outweigh any minuses. Prefabs tend to be both cheaper and quicker to build than conventional homes, creating more affordable buildings, while the reduced time spent on site in combination with high standards of insulation help reduce the impact on the environment. One of the greatest challenges for architects and designers lies in the fact that standardized, prefabricated homes are seldom site-specific, requiring a degree of flexibility and adaptability in the plan to allow the building to sit neatly and responsively within all kinds of contexts. This was very much the approach to the design of the Plus House.

'At first glance, Plus House is a typical traditional Swedish house, with the proportions taken from the generic Swedish barn,' says architect Mårten Claesson. 'Up close, however, it is quite extreme, with either complete glazing or fully closed walls and a total reduction of detail. To achieve this balancing act was more difficult than might at first appear. The house was not designed for this site, but in fact the setting could not have suited it better.'

The house is situated about a 20-minute drive from Stockholm, close to a small, rural village and a nature reserve. The clients were living in an apartment in the city, but wanted more space for themselves and their two children. Having found the perfect location, they approached the prefabrication specialists Arkitekthus and chose one of two designs developed for the company by the architects (another collaboration is Folded Roof House; p. 100). The chosen design takes its name from the key sightlines that pass through the upper and lower levels of the house, one from front to back (ground floor) and the other from side to side (upper floor). On a diagram combining the two levels, these indicators fuse into a plus sign. These sightlines and the extensive use of banks of triple-glazing allow a significant degree of connectivity with the landscape, with the building neatly adapting to this rural setting, bordered by pine trees and rocky outcrops.

The ground floor is semi-open plan, with walls of glass opening out onto a long timber deck. Within, a seating area sits to one side of the staircase; to the other is the kitchen and dining area. A separate service and utility zone is located behind the kitchen at the far end of the house. Upstairs, the bedrooms sit to either side of the staircase and a central bathroom, with enough space for a fitted desk in one of the two long landings that extend all the way to the integrated balconies at either end. Fitted storage cupboards are also hosted by these landings.

Constructed with factory-made component panels and parts, this house of spruce, steel and glass was assembled on site in 20 days. 'All three represent local Swedish materials that are available at a reasonable cost,' Claesson adds. 'Plus House has many virtues and, apart from being a fantastic living machine for a family, it is also humble and proof of the potential for creating good architecture on a low budget.'

The ground-floor living spaces open up to adjoining terraces, and bring the landscape into the house. The palette for the interiors is relatively minimal, allowing the focus to remain on the views.

Country Homes   Plus House

The house's pared-down exterior and pitched roof echo the form of a barn, as well as playing with imaginative contrasts between mass and transparency.

Villa G

Skanderborg, Denmark

C. F. Møller

One of the most romantic of residential typologies, the Scandinavian farmhouse still has particular resonance in rural settings. The architectural practice C. F. Møller, founded in the 1920s, recently reinterpreted the notion of the Danish farmstead in the form of Villa G, a live/work building with a series of interconnected, single-storey structures, arranged around a central courtyard. The house is located in Skanderborg, a semi-rural enclave southwest of Aarhus, and the site itself is delightful and engaging, with open pasture all around bordered by mature woodland, not far from the Gudenå river.

The new building, designed by Mads Møller and his associates, replaces a former smallholding that comprised four distinct wings. The old farm offered a key point of reference, yet the new building of brick and slate is distinctly contemporary in form and character. 'The materials were chosen for their qualities of durability and being able to blend into the natural surroundings,' says architect Julian Weyer. 'But they also lend the simple building volumes a rich, tactile quality, which are appreciated as the house is approached. The project was a chance to explore spatial richness and propose a modern, bright and innovative Scandinavian interpretation of a classic hunting lodge.'

One of the wings of the house is devoted to a multipurpose space, originally designed to serve as a workshop and office, while the wing opposite holds the family's private quarters, comprising four bedrooms and two bathrooms. Between the two sits a sequence of living spaces, with the kitchen and dining area at the heart of the floorplan. Central 'cracked-roof' skylights are used periodically to help lift the quality of light, while the interiors are defined by wooden floors, brick fireplaces and crisp, white walls and ceilings. A separate structure holds the garage and plant room, helping to encircle and protect the central courtyard. The landscape design, also by the architects, enhances the ideal of a farmhouse floating in an open meadow, with the fields meeting the house without any formal borderland. A combination of wood-burning stoves plus geothermal heating helps to reinforce the environmental sensitivity and green credentials of the project.

'The clients were looking for a modern take on a classic rural typology, but not in a nostalgic way,' Weyer adds. 'We wanted to make the building fit well into the location and enable a modern lifestyle that includes running a small rural business. There is no doubt that this is a distinctly Nordic setting, but the structure of the family rooms is also very Scandinavian in feel, combining the large, open shared spaces with more private rooms in a way that offers autonomy to all members of the family.'

The main living spaces flow one into another within a vibrant *promenade architecturale*. With height and light, these are inviting rooms, connecting to the open landscape.

Sitting within an open meadow, the villa offers a modern interpretation of the farmstead, drawing upon vernacular references and such traditional materials as brick and timber.

Villa Sunnanö

Borlänge, Sweden

Murman Arkitekter

Creating and then curating a vivid sense of connection with the landscape is a key priority in the design of Nordic rural houses. The beauty of the countryside inspires a powerful response among contemporary Scandinavian architects, including Hans Murman, whose buildings display a considered sensitivity to the natural world. This is certainly true of Villa Sunnanö, which offers multiple lenses focused on the dramatic and enticing lakeside setting.

The clients asked for a new home, not far from the town of Borlänge, around 225 km (140 miles) northwest of Stockholm. The site itself, already inhabited by a cabin and a host of mature trees, sits on a promontory pushing out into the lake. The risk of flooding means that houses here have to be lifted a metre (a little over 3 ft) above ground level, but the need to establish a series of sightlines that would take full advantage of the views was also a priority. 'We wanted to create a place for nature lovers, given that the location is suitable for boating and swimming, as well as skating and skiing in the winter,' Murman explains. 'The clients also liked the idea of sheltered patios from morning to evening, and materials for the façade that would adapt to the surrounding landscape.'

Veering away from the idea of a traditional rectilinear cabin, Murman created a more complex form that maximizes the different views of the lake and the landscape. In plan, the ground floor takes the form of a six-pointed star, with the points each facing a different direction and the majority featuring gables with floor-to-ceiling glass, leading to sheltered verandas. All of the key living spaces are contained within this formation, arranged around a central hallway, with a blend of open-plan spaces and more contained areas, including a gym.

An elongated, covered bridge floats over this 'star' at an upper level, which contains most of the bedrooms and creates a strong axis line sheltering the entrance area below, as well as an additional porch facing the lake. This projecting bridge reinforces an axial line that continues outside and connects with a dock, which pushes out into the water. The existing cabin was also refurbished to serve as a garage and storage space. The wood façade is complemented by a *faltak*, or a sculptural unity. Treated with iron sulphate, the wood assumes a grey tone that helps it blend into the surrounding landscape. The subtlety and uniformity of the materials also act as an aid to offset the complex geometry of the building.

'The house melts into the environment in a way that makes it feel as if it has always been there,' say the clients. 'We love the views and the beauty of the detailing.'

The star-shaped geometry of the house defines the various interior spaces. The main living zones on the ground floor filter outwards from the central hallway, which also hosts the stairway.

The composition is abstract and engaging, yet also plays with familiar ideas and natural materials. The 'star' formation offers a series of framed panoramas, including from the elevated bridge on the upper level.

Slutterupgård

Hørsholm, Denmark

Henning Larsen

The challenge posed by Michael Ring, the owner of the Danish design and homeware brand Stelton, and his wife Birgitte to their architects was to create not just a new country house, but also a 21st-century farm. The couple, whose 58-acre farm is largely devoted to breeding horses, approached the esteemed architectural practice founded by the Danish master Henning Larsen in 1959 and which is still flourishing today. 'Our goal was to create a unique farm with low or zero-fossil energy consumption,' Ring explains. 'It was pivotal that the wood was sourced locally in Scandinavia and, as many minimalistic houses can seem cold and a bit harsh, we wanted a home that was warm and welcoming.'

The farm sits within the municipality of Hørsholm, a picturesque district close to the Øresund coast and just 25 km (16 miles) from Copenhagen. Architect Søren Øllgaard embraced the brief set by the clients to create a modern farmstead in harmony with this gently undulating landscape of pasture and woodland. The new buildings comprise stables for around 20 horses, service buildings and an indoor riding arena, arranged in an L-shaped formation around a dressage field, with the black composite panels of the façades lending the collection of structures a graphic and complementary identity. The stabled horses help generate heat for an adjoining apartment for farm staff, and solar panels create electricity for the entire farm in combination with a ground-source heat pump.

The farmhouse sits on the brow of a modest slope, overlooking the equine courtyard and the farm. The vital connections with the surrounding landscape have been enhanced by elevating the building a little further on the hillside, with garaging and service spaces tucked beneath the main body of the building. The upper storey is mostly devoted to partially open-plan living spaces, including a seating zone at one end and a central kitchen and dining area, which also lead out to an adjoining terrace. The master suite sits to the rear of the house, which is bordered by a balcony that runs along one side and round to an elevated veranda overlooking the farm below.

'We are pleased to have created a project that is fully consistent, including residence, stables and riding arena,' says Øllgaard. 'The farm is integrated into the landscape and is accessible to nature in a way that is very characteristic of the Scandinavian way of life and its architecture.'

Country Homes Slutterupgård

An elevated piano nobile provides a vantage point across the farm and the landscape. The integrated hearth forms both a focal point and a partial partition between the kitchen/dining area and the living space/library.

The house offers a series of complementary
outdoor rooms, including a terrace to one
side and an integrated veranda to the front.

Store Lauvøya-Bestemorstua

Storlauvøya, Norway

Mikado Arkitektur

When Roar Henden was a child, growing up on the western coast of Norway, the island of Storlauvøya, southwest of Trondheim, was only accessible by boat. Today, however, the famous Atlantic Ocean Road, an extraordinary stretch of highway completed in 1989, ties together a string of islands, including Storlauvøya, via a series of causeways and bridges. Regarded as one of the best road trips in Scandinavia, the road has also encouraged fresh settlers, including Henden, his wife Linda Kristin and their two children, who now live on the island full time.

'I have always loved Storlauvøya, and when a house came up for sale here I was lucky enough to buy it,' he says. 'At the time we were living in Oslo, but moving to the island seemed the most natural thing in the world to do. It is a very special place for children to grow up in, surrounded by the sea, nature and farm animals, while at the same time only minutes away from a village with a school. We love the fact that our home is in such a remote location, yet is so close to a community with everything we might need.'

The house was a late 19th-century building known as 'Bestemorstua', and the family embraced local planning restrictions that insisted upon full-time residency. Having a strong interest in architecture, both traditional and contemporary, Henden was keen to extend the modestly scaled structure, creating extra living space and room for visiting guests, and turned to architect Mika Meienberger of Mikado Arkitektur. Working around a series of planning conditions, which included restrictions on the height of any extension and insistence on the presence of a pitched roof, she came up with the idea of a new twin for the old cottage.

This new structure would be distinctly contemporary, set slightly apart from and behind the older house, with a modest bridging zone between the two. 'I wanted to explore the architectural affinities between new and old, and the interconnection of spaces,' Meienberger explains. 'The idea was to create a nonidentical twin, with its own character, placed side by side with the original house. Like yin and yang, the two parts would complement each other, visually and practically. The slate-covered extension sits like a rock next to its twin, anchoring it to the ground and protecting it from the strong sea winds.'

In the older part of the house, the interiors were refreshed, updated and opened out, and links to the new portion were staggered through stepped changes in floor level, reinforcing the partition between old and new. New bedrooms were created at ground level and on the upper storey, while a basement contains a family den and exercise room. The result is a substantial family home, which has delighted Henden. 'We feel that the soul of the original house has been preserved,' he says, 'even though we have also created something completely new and modern.'

Country Homes

Store Lauvøya-Bestemorstua

The house is a fusion of old and new, with the link between them offering an entrance hall plus a staircase to one side. The main living spaces are in the original part of the house, with bathrooms and bedrooms situated in the new extension.

House Riihi

Alajärvi, Finland

OOPEAA

Over recent years, the concept of the compound house has gained increasing traction. Comprising a small number of complementary structures, it offers a range of bespoke spaces suited to different functions and purposes, while providing the opportunity for both private retreats and more open and communal living areas. There is a clear overlap, or point of connection, with the notion of the farmstead, which helped to provide the inspiration for the design of this home in rural Finland by architect Anssi Lassila of OOPEAA.

Situated around 400 km (250 miles) north of Helsinki, the setting is rural, with a context of farmland and woods around the borders of Lake Alajärvi. The house was commissioned by a couple – an entrepreneur and an artist – who required both a home and office/studio spaces. 'They wanted a house that would serve the individual needs of each person, while serving the family as a whole,' explains Lassila. 'They also wanted a building that would be ecologically sustainable and work in harmony with the surroundings. The composition recalls the arrangement of a traditional Finnish farm, in which wooden cottages form a protective inner courtyard with the buildings facing onto it.'

The house comprises three separate structures that help to protect and shelter the cobbled courtyard, complete with a sandpit and play space at its heart. An L-shaped master building, holding the family living spaces and bedrooms, is complemented by a separate atelier, while a third building serves as a garage plus workshop. The collection of structures share the same architectural language, with cladding of local spruce and pitched roofs in aluminium.

Spatially, each building is tailored to need and function. The atelier, for instance, is a largely open space with high ceilings and a rich quality of natural light; a wall of glass at one gable end offers picture-book views of the open landscape. The main house offers a combination of open-plan living space, as well as a master suite in one wing and the children's bedrooms in the other. Heating is provided by four wood-burning stoves, which also heat hot water, while electricity comes from battery storage fed by a solar array. In this way, the house can function off-grid, while all the construction materials, including the aluminium, were sourced locally.

'For me, the most satisfying aspect of the completed building is the way that it enters into a dialogue with the surrounding landscape,' Lassila adds. 'The fact that we were able to create a house that can provide enough heat and electricity for its own needs in our Nordic climate is particularly satisfying.'

Country Homes

House Riihi

The main living spaces and bedrooms sit within an L-shaped building that looks out to open landscape at one side and a courtyard at the other. All of the materials used for the crafted interiors were sourced locally.

Together with a studio and garage/
workshop, the house is part of a triptych of
single-storey structures arranged around a
central courtyard, echoing the formation of
traditional Finnish farmhouses.

Villa Blåbär

Nacka, Sweden

PS Arkitektur

In many parts of Scandinavia, the idea of a black house has particular resonance. Traditional cabins, wooden houses and fishermen's huts were often protected with a layer of black pine tar or, sometimes, a dark mineral-based paint; variations on such a treatment can be seen on barns and farm buildings in England and in other parts of northern Europe. Architect Peter Sahlin has explored the idea of the black house in a number of projects, including his own rural getaway in Lapland. For Villa Blåbär, he has given the black cottage, or cabin, a particular twist.

The house was clad not with timber treated with tar or paint, but with black roofing felt. This, together with the modern shape and form of the building, ensures that it stands out to graphic effect in the winter months, when the contrast with a snowy backdrop becomes vivid. The choice of material also echoes the common vernacular, and reinforces the more contemporary nature of the architecture, while helping to reduce costs. 'When designing private villas and ski cabins, we always try to balance the vernacular part with a more inventive part,' Sahlin explains. 'In some areas of Sweden, the vernacular approach is more expected, but in others, like here, it is less important. We always challenge the obvious and look for something unique.'

The setting of the villa has a distinctly rural feel, surrounded by mature trees, with rocky outcrops that help to define the rugged topography. Located within the municipality of Nacka, the house is actually just a short distance from Stockholm, sitting within the inner part of the capital's epic archipelago, which itself offers an enticing escape for many city dwellers. For Karl and Sofia Andersson, together with their three young children, it serves as a full-time residence. The couple wanted to create a home that was bold and daring architecturally, but also energy-efficient and environmentally friendly. It was important that the building should connect to the landscape in an easy and immediate way. The budget was relatively modest, hence the decision to use some low-cost materials, including the roofing felt for the façade.

The house floats a few feet above the irregular granite rocks below, supported on a series of concrete piloti, which help to create a stable platform in a subtle zigzag formation. Much of the building is single storey, with the exception of a den that sits in a loft at one end, rather like a lookout post or ship's bridge. On the main level, open-plan living spaces sit at the heart of the building, with an easily accessible terrace to one side. The kitchen and service spaces lie at one end of the house, with the family bedrooms at the other. The master bedroom, in particular, is orientated for striking views of the surrounding woodland, lending the house something of a treehouse feel, reinforced by the sense of being elevated above the rocks.

Country Homes   Villa Blåbär

The house offers a striking contrast between the black exterior and the vivid white interiors. The main living spaces are at one end of the house, with a long hallway leading to the bedrooms.

Villa N1

Frösakull, Sweden

Jonas Lindvall A & D

The organic beauty of natural materials has always been a key component of Scandinavian architecture, forming a vital aspect of its essential character. Of all of these materials, the one that we most readily associate with the Nordic house is wood, which has been explored to great effect in the design for Villa N1 by Jonas Lindvall. 'We decided that we wanted to make something deeply rooted in the vernacular,' he says. 'The challenge was to make something that is modern yet linked to the history of the region, which appears to be quite humble from the outside, but becomes something different once you enter it.'

The timber barns found in this part of southwestern Sweden, with their simple and pleasing outlines, were particular sources of reference. As one approaches the closed entrance to one side of the building, it does indeed have the enigmatic appearance of an abstract modern barn, with a path leading to a wooden door in a wooden façade, topped by a pitched roof, which is also made from untreated oak. Yet a key part of Lindvall's thinking about this house, which was designed as a summer retreat for a family with three children, was that it should offer a process of unfolding discovery.

True to this idea, the building reveals itself gradually as a far more complex entity, comprising five interconnected, single-storey barn-style pavilions, arranged in a staggered sequence, with a number of shifts in size and scale that become clearer as one travels through the complex. Bedrooms for the family and visiting guests are placed within three pavilions at opposite ends of the sequence; the largest of these modern 'barns' also features a family den. The communal living areas, comprising a kitchen and dining pavilion, with a sitting room alongside, sit within a more open and social zone at the centre. Within this part of the house, glazing has been used much more extensively, with sliding-glass walls in the gable ends leading out onto both a sheltered veranda and terraces defined by sandstone pavers. Sandstone has also been used throughout, establishing a contrast with the relative simplicity of the timber shell. In the bathroom and the kitchen, the use of Carrara marble reinforces the crafted and beautifully detailed quality of the villa.

'The house has a number of different layers, so that not everything is immediately apparent,' Lindvall explains. 'It also feels very harmonious. I wanted it to feel like a favourite jacket that fits really well.'

The main living spaces are at the centre of the villa, with bedrooms and bathrooms pushed out to the wings at either end. These key zones feed out onto a veranda and terraces, reinforcing the strong sense of connection between indoors and out.

Country Homes   Villa N1

Split View Mountain Lodge

Geilo, Norway

Reiulf Ramstad Arkitekter

One of the greatest strengths of Nordic architecture is its highly contextual approach. Houses and buildings are crafted according to the landscape and topography with sensitivity and care. In this sense, the architecture of the region is organic in its thoughtfulness and consideration for the environment. In rural contexts, of course, this approach becomes even more important, as was the case with the design and build of Split View Mountain Lodge in the Norwegian county of Buskerud.

'We believe that building in the landscape is something that must be done with respect,' says architect Reiulf Ramstad. 'This house represents a very tailored response to its surroundings. In all of our designs, we believe strongly that the foundation for a building is the place itself. When we saw the site, we realized it had a number of different qualities we wanted to respond to.'

The lodge sits in the mountain resort of Havsdalen, near Geilo, an area renowned for its skiing and hiking. It is also a place of extremes. The clients, who have three children, requested a new mountainside home for themselves and visiting family and friends. Recognizing that a holiday home of this kind has different requirements to a house for daily living, both architect and clients reduced the programme to a relatively modest scale – somewhat dictated by the necessity of completing construction within the window offered by the summer months – while making the most of the location. The timber-clad house is accessed via a small basement level, tucked into the hillside and largely devoted to storage and services, while also forming a kind of plinth for the main body of the building above. Here, the floorplan is, in part, a response to key vistas of the mountain ranges across the valley.

The linear portion of the house holds the family bedrooms, plus a den for the children; beyond this, it forks in a Y-shaped formation pointing towards the open views. The kitchen sits within the circulation axis at the heart of the building, with four steps leading up to a dining area in one part of the split and a lounge in the other, both featuring gable ends of floor-to-ceiling glass. The key material throughout is untreated pine, with many features – including the kitchen, storage and window seats – bespoke and built-in. The house is heated by a combination of wood-burning stoves and geothermal heat pump. A separate annexe forms a complementary and self-contained unit for guests, allowing a degree of privacy for hosts and visitors.

'In the end, we managed to obtain more with less, which is an important part of sustainability,' Ramstad explains. 'When you have a smaller programme, you can strengthen the impact of the indoor–outdoor spaces, and let the light and the views play a bigger role in how you live within them.'

The principal material for the interiors is pine, which gives the house a warm, natural feel. Among the many integrated pieces of furniture are window seats and fitted benches.

The bespoke kitchen sits at the hub of the house, where the piano nobile splits into two, with one section holding the dining area and the other the lounge, both heated by wood-burning stoves.

The guest annexe is semi-independent from the rest of the house, and has its own seating area with a sofa bed, bathroom and mezzanine sleeping platform.

Villa Moelven

Stockholm, Sweden

Arkitektstudio Widjedal Racki

Challenged to create a 'showcase for wood', many architects would resort to simple forms, modern variants on the cabin, farmhouse, barn or fisherman's cottage. Architects Håkon Widjedal and Natasha Racki, however, opted for a more imaginative approach in their design for Villa Moelven. Instead of low-slung simplicity, this timber-clad home features three main storeys of living space, layered with considerable spatial and volumetric complexity. The architects liken the house to a labyrinth: rich in natural light and texture, and offering a complex journey of discovery, as one circulates through the variety of fluid spaces within the building.

'The clients' desire for surprising spaces led us into an investigation of the labyrinth,' Widjedal explains. 'With the aid of many models, we tested the idea of experiences and functions as a continuous flow, rather than dividing them up into separate spaces. In the finished building, there are seven different floor levels and eleven stairways. Many rooms and passageways are hidden initially, so that they are gradually discovered by the visitor. It is the perfect house for playing hide and seek.'

The house itself, located in a rural enclave within Stockholm's inner archipelago, was commissioned by a family with two children. But the project was also a collaboration with one of the largest timber companies in Scandinavia – Moelven – which has a range of sawmills across the region. The villa represented an opportunity to promote the dexterity of timber as an architectural material, while moving beyond archetypal wooden houses. It sits on a rugged foundation of bare rock, which gives the house a gently elevated position within the landscape and accentuates the views through the trees to the water.

At times, the wooden terraces, balconies and vertical latticed sunscreens, which border and protect the house, work around the vast chunks of granite that help to define the setting and its topography. Above the rock, around 98 per cent of the house is made of wood, with the exterior cladding made from heat-treated pine. The structural framework was made from a grid of glulam beams, prefabricated to order and pieced together on site. Plywood was used extensively for the interior panelling.

Simply put, the entrance, service areas and family spaces are at ground level, the main living area at mid-level and family bedrooms and a library on the upper storey, yet the concept of a fluid labyrinth means that the interiors are far more complex, featuring many integrated elements along the way, from bookcases to storage niches and hideaways. The combination of warm, exposed timber and the alternating sequence of open spaces and more intimate zones suggests an abstract alpine chalet, uprooted and placed by the waters of the archipelago.

Country Homes   Villa Moelven

The exterior spaces immediately around the house are home to a series of decks, terraces and balconies on multiple levels, which serve as a continuation and integral part of the overall composition.

The many shifts and changes in floor level and volume give the interiors a labyrinthine quality. In some cases, these junctions provide opportunities for integrated seating that morphs into steps within a highly bespoke approach.

Country Homes

Villa Moelven

Plans

Norderhov Cabin

Hønefoss, Norway

Atelier Oslo

p. 14

1 Plan
2 Axonometric
3 Section

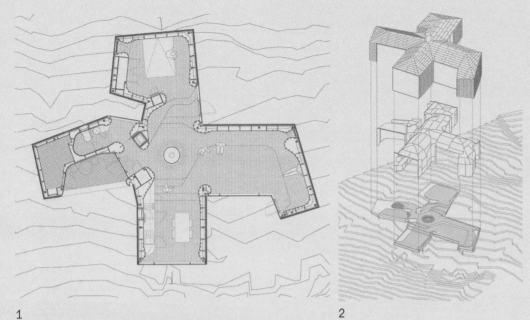

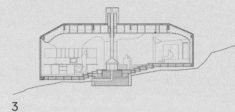

3

1

2

Cabin Ustaoset

Ustaoset, Norway

Jon Danielsen Aarhus

p. 20

1 Sections
2 Plans

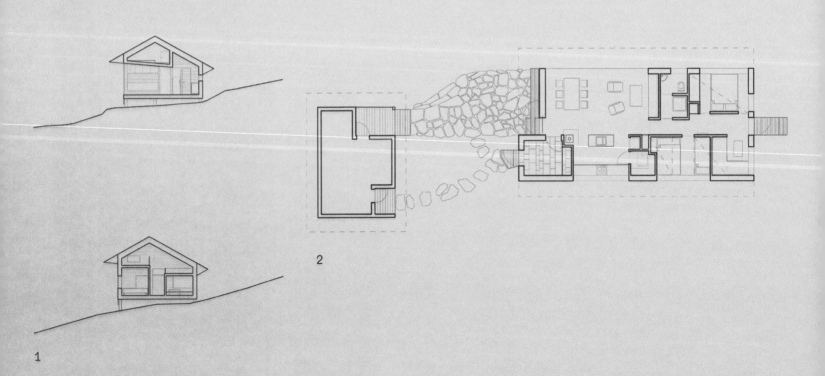

2

1

Gotland Summerhouse

Gotland, Sweden

Enflo Arkitekter & DEVE Architects

p. 28

1 Plans
2 Section
3 Elevation

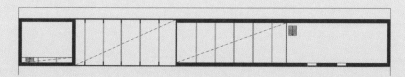

1

2

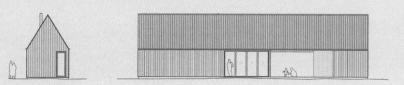

3

Gudbrandslie Cabin

Tyinkrysset, Norway

Helen & Hard

p. 34

1 First-floor plan
2 Basement plan
3 Elevations

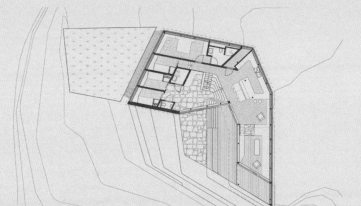

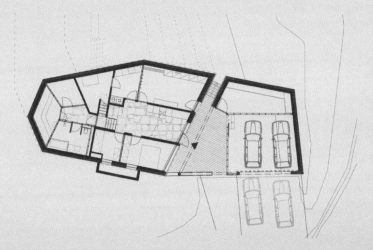

1

2

SOUTH

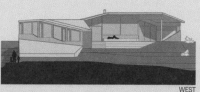
WEST

NORTH

3

Plans

Hytte Hvasser

Hvasser, Norway

Hille Strandskogen Architects

p. 40

1 Ground-floor plan
2 First-floor plan

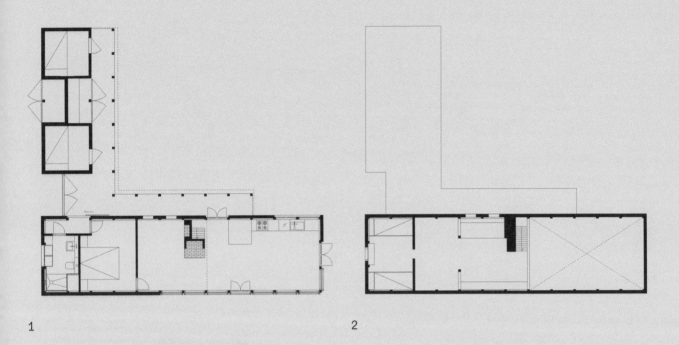

1

2

Villa Buresø

Slangerup, Denmark

Mette Lange Architects

p. 46

1 Plan

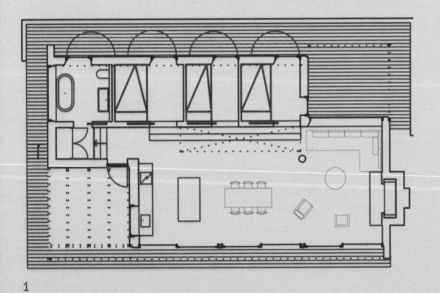

1

Bungenäs, Sweden

1

2

Plans

Bjellandsbu-Åkrafjorden Cabin   Etne, Norway   Snøhetta

p. 60

1 Elevation
2 Elevation

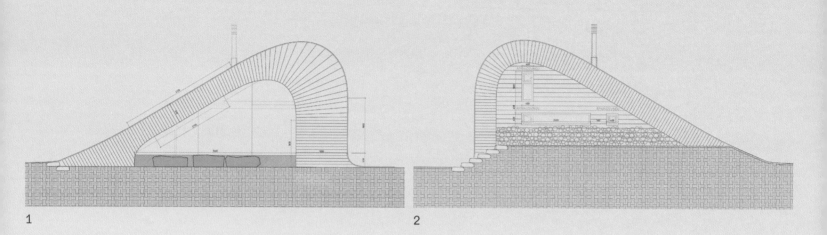

1

2

Arctic Treehouse Hotel   Rovaniemi, Finland   Studio Puisto

p. 66

1 Restaurant plan
2 Floorplan (type 1)
3 Floorplan (type 2)

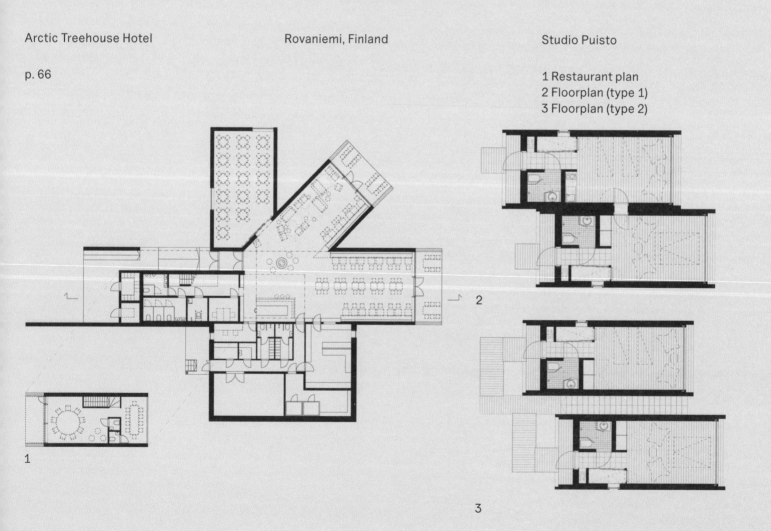

1

2

3

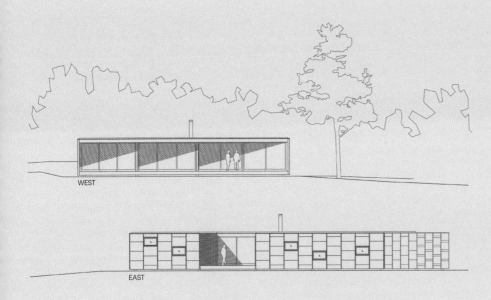

WEST

EAST

NORTH

1

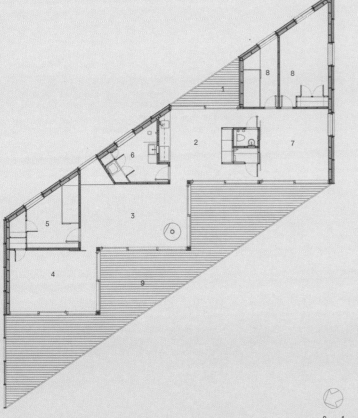

1. ENTRANCE
2. KITCHEN
3. LIVING ROOM
4. MASTER BEDROOM
5. CHILDREN'S ROOM
6. BATHROOM / LAUNDRY
7. STUDIO
8. GUEST ROOM
9. TERRACE / WOODEN TRELLIS

0   1   5   10

2

Plans

Cabin Vindheim   Sjoga, Norway   Vardehaugen

p. 78   1 Sections

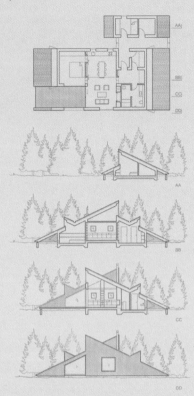

1

Åre Solbringen   Åre, Sweden   Waldemarson Berglund Arkitekter

p. 84   1 Site plan
                                                                               2 Plan + section

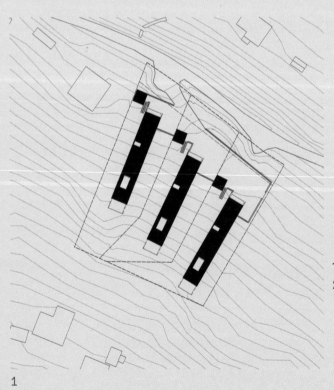

1

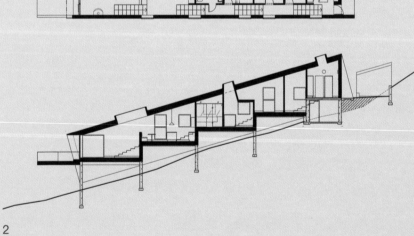

2

1 Plans
2 Sections

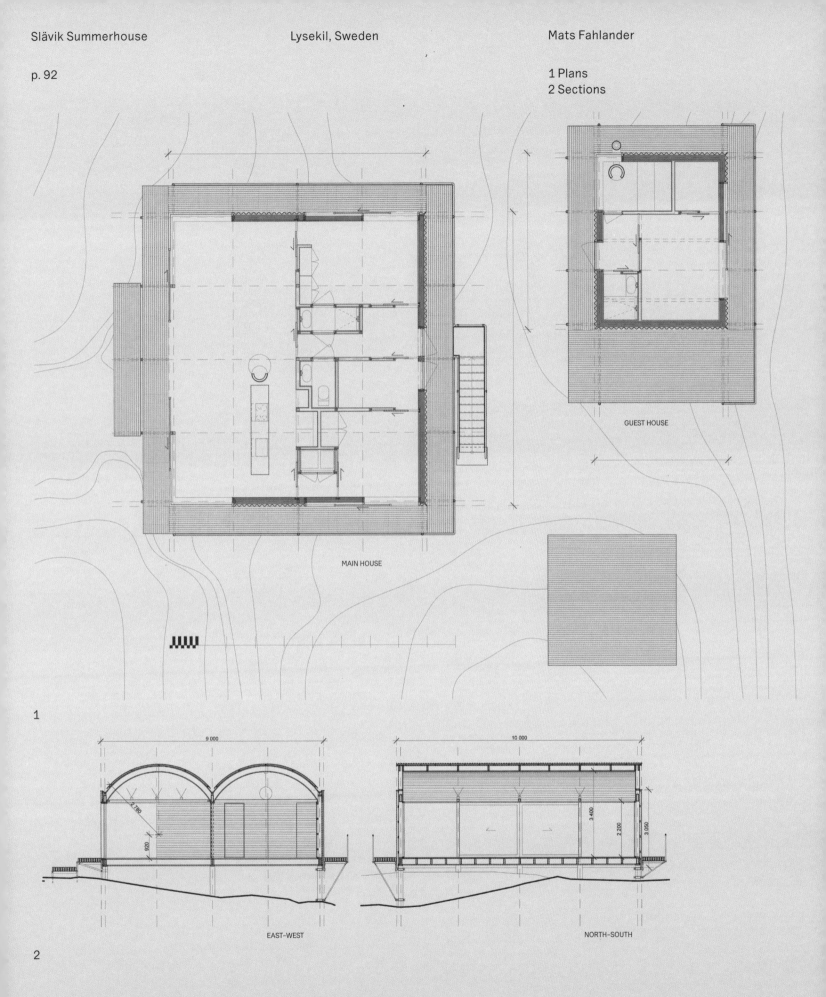

GUEST HOUSE

MAIN HOUSE

1

9 000

2 180

920

EAST–WEST

10 000

3 400

2 200

3 050

NORTH–SOUTH

2

Plans

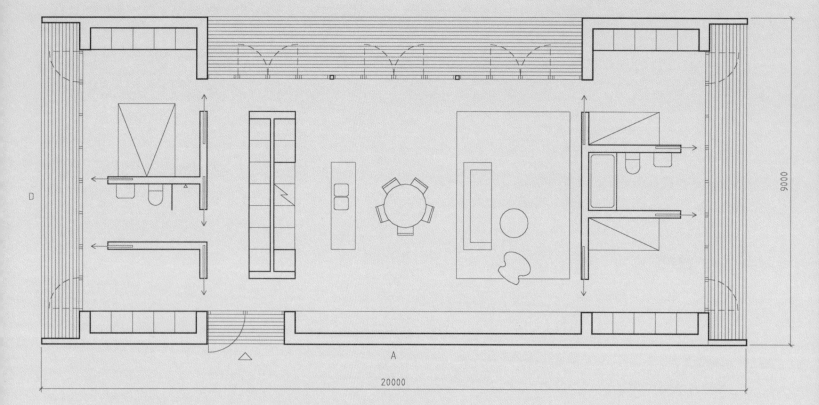

9000

20000

1

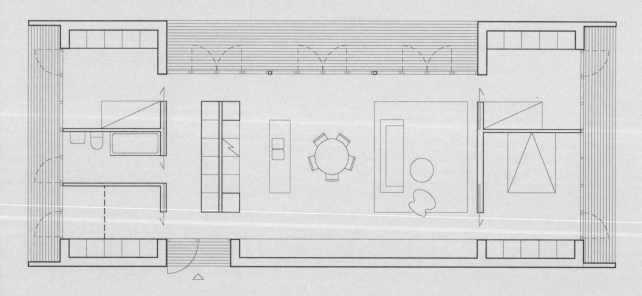

2

Aluminium Cabin

p. 108

Nøtterøy, Norway

Jarmund/Vigsnæs Arkitekter

1 Plan
2 Section
3 Site plan

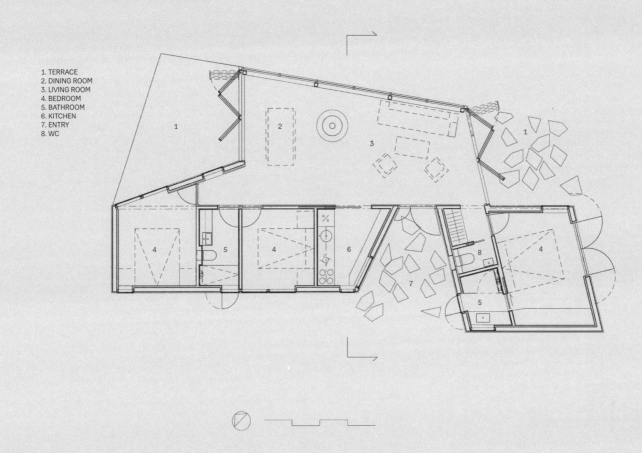

1. TERRACE
2. DINING ROOM
3. LIVING ROOM
4. BEDROOM
5. BATHROOM
6. KITCHEN
7. ENTRY
8. WC

1

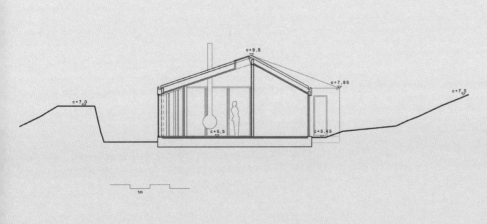

2

3

Plans

Split House   Asker, Norway   Jarmund/Vigsnæs Arkitekter

p. 114   1 Ground-floor plan
                                                               2 Lower ground-floor plan

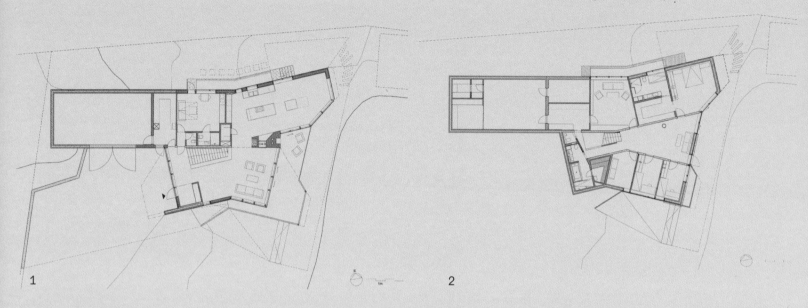

1   2

Weekend House   Sildegarnsholmen, Norway   Knut Hjeltnes Sivilarkitekter

p. 120   1 Plans
                                                               2 Sections

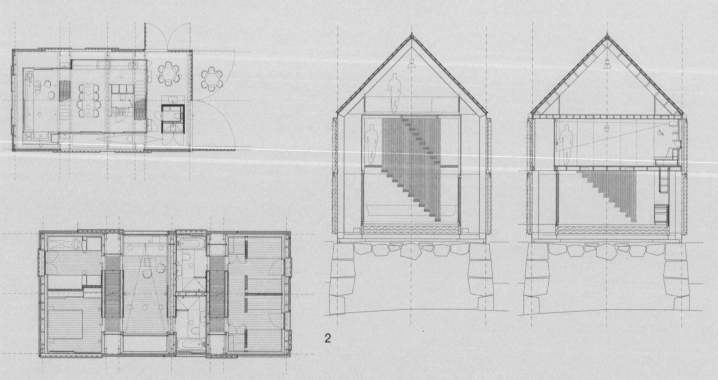

2

1

Vega Hytte

p. 124

Vega, Norway

Kolman Boye Architects

1 Plan
2 Section

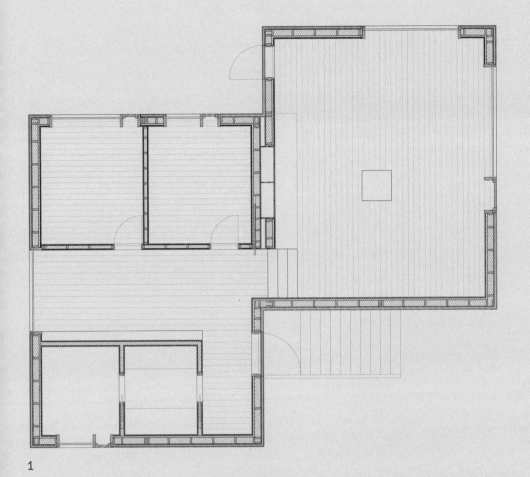

1

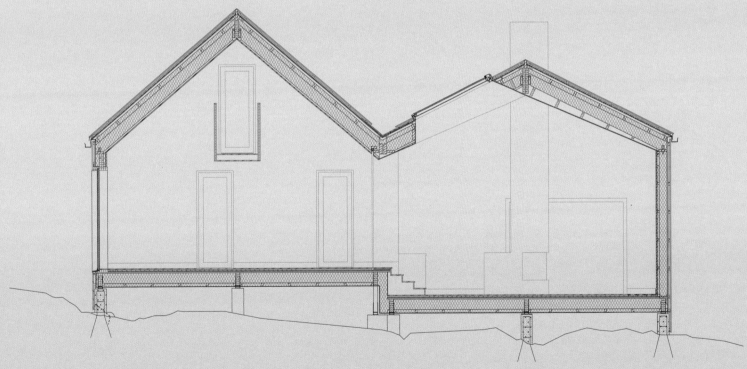

2

Plans

Lille Arøya

p. 130

Larvik, Norway

Lund Hagem Architects

1 Elevations
2 Site plan
3 Sections

SOUTH

EAST

NORTH

WEST

1

2

3

Stupet

p. 136

Omberg, Sweden

Petra Gipp Arkitektur

1 Plan
2 Elevations

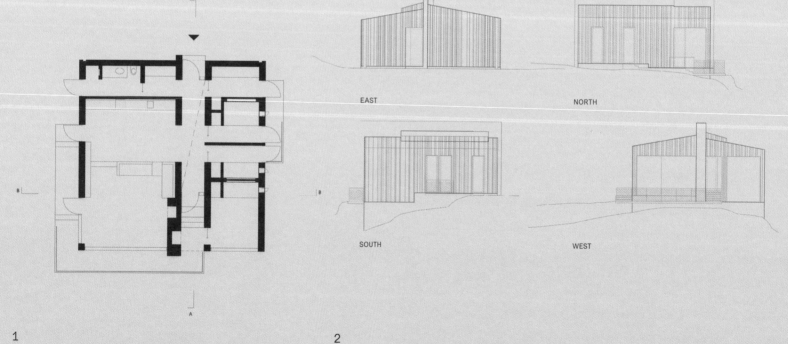

EAST

NORTH

SOUTH

WEST

1

2

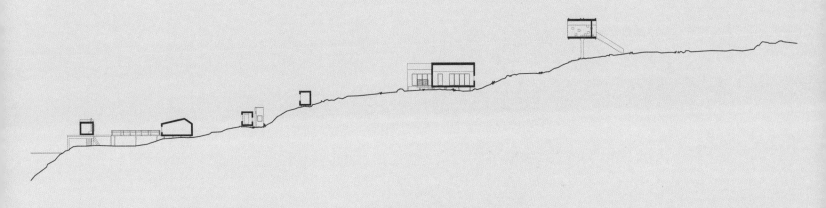

1

Manshausen Island Resort

p. 150

Steigen, Norway

Stinessen Arkitektur

1 Plan

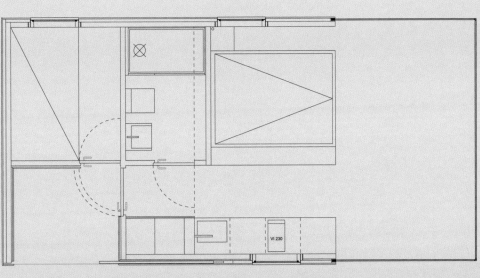

VI 230

1

Stockholm, Sweden

Tham & Videgård

p. 156

1 Plan
2 Axonometric

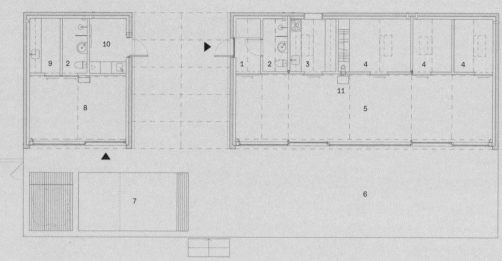

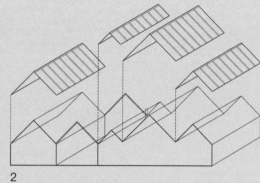

1. ENTRANCE
2. WC
3. KITCHEN
4. BEDROOM
5. LIVING/DINING ROOM
6. TERRACE
7. POOL
8. GUEST ROOM/STUDIO
9. PANTRY
10. TECHNICAL ROOM
11. HEATER

2

1

Villa Björnberget

Nacka, Sweden

Delin Arkitektkontor

p. 164

1 Plan
2 Elevations

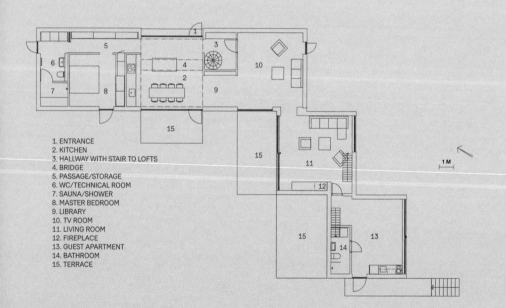

NORTHWEST

SOUTHEAST

1. ENTRANCE
2. KITCHEN
3. HALLWAY WITH STAIR TO LOFTS
4. BRIDGE
5. PASSAGE/STORAGE
6. WC/TECHNICAL ROOM
7. SAUNA/SHOWER
8. MASTER BEDROOM
9. LIBRARY
10. TV ROOM
11. LIVING ROOM
12. FIREPLACE
13. GUEST APARTMENT
14. BATHROOM
15. TERRACE

1 M

2

1

Townhouse

Landskrona, Sweden

Elding Oscarson

p. 172

1 Plans

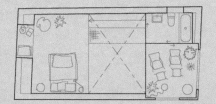

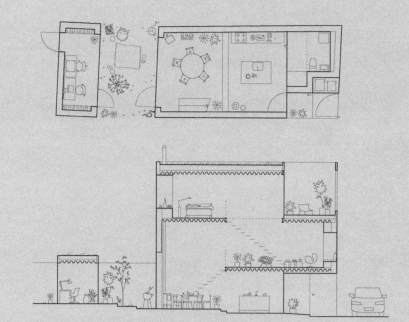

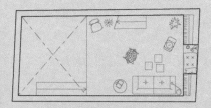

1

Mölle by the Sea

Mölle, Sweden

Elding Oscarson

p. 178

1 Ground-floor plan
2 Upper-floor + basement plan

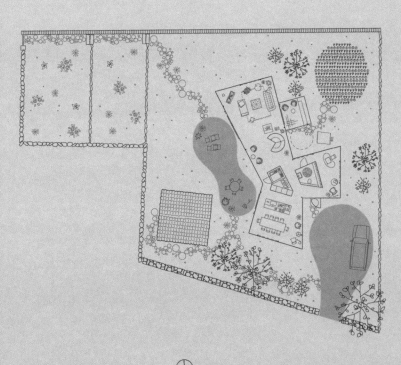

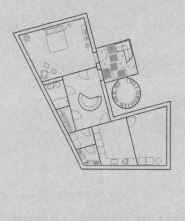

2

1

Plans

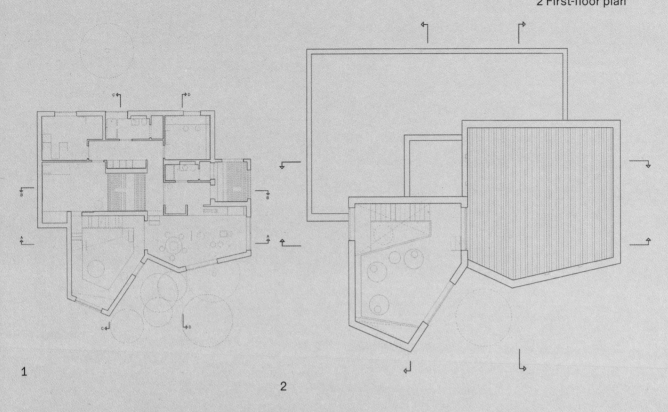

1

2

Villa S   Bergen, Norway   Saunders Architecture

p. 190   1 Ground-floor plan
                                                                         2 First-floor plan
                                                                         3 Second-floor plan

1. ENTRANCE
2. TV ROOM
3. STORAGE 1
4. STORAGE 2
5. OUTDOOR AREA
6. FIREPLACE

1. OUTDOOR AREA
2. LIBRARY
3. BOOKSHELF
4. OUTDOOR AREA
5. ROOF WITH TABLE

1

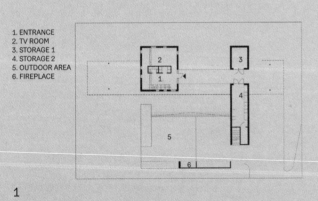

1. BALCONY
2. LIVING ROOM
3. FIREPLACE
4. BEDROOM
5. BEDROOM
6. BATHROOM
7. LAUNDRY
8. KITCHEN
9. CLOSET
10. BALCONY
11. BEDROOM
12. CLOSET
13. BATHROOM

3

2

Roof House

Copenhagen, Denmark

Sigurd Larsen

p. 196

1 Elevations
2 Plan

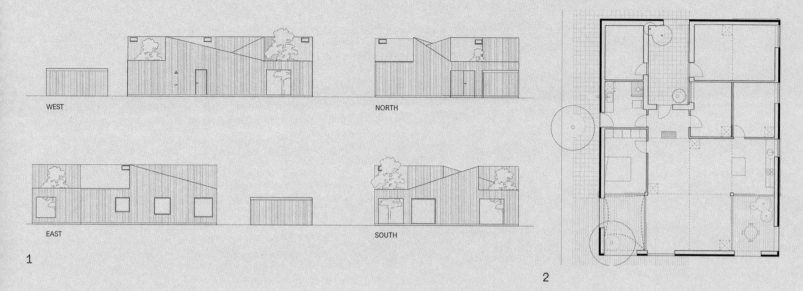

WEST

NORTH

EAST

SOUTH

1

2

Villa R

Ljungskile, Sweden

Arkitekterna Krook & Tjäder

p. 202

1 Plans

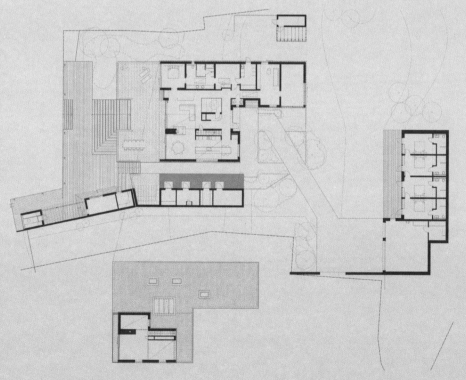

1

Plans

Villa Kristina

Gothenburg, Sweden

Wingårdh Arkitektkontor

p. 208

1 First-floor plan
2 Ground-floor plan
3 Elevation

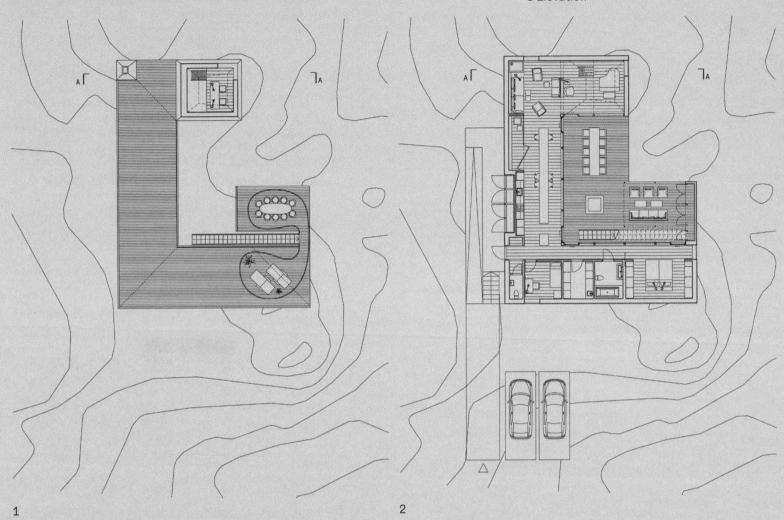

1

2

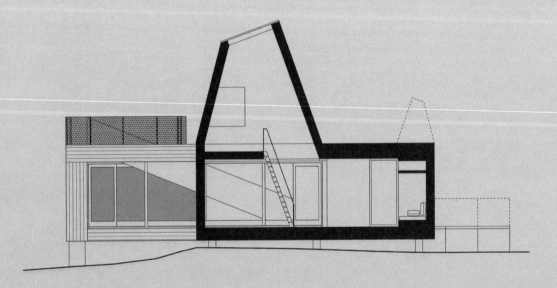

3

1 First-floor plan
2 Ground-floor plan
3 Elevation

Four Cornered Villa

p. 216

Virrat, Finland

Avanto Architects

1 Elevations
2 Plan

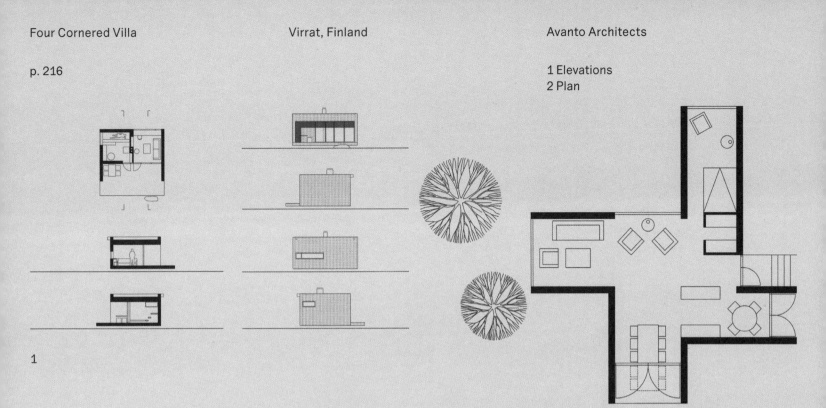

1

2

House for a Drummer

p. 222

Kärna, Sweden

Bornstein Lyckefors Architects

1 Ground-floor plan
2 First-floor plan
3 Second-floor plan

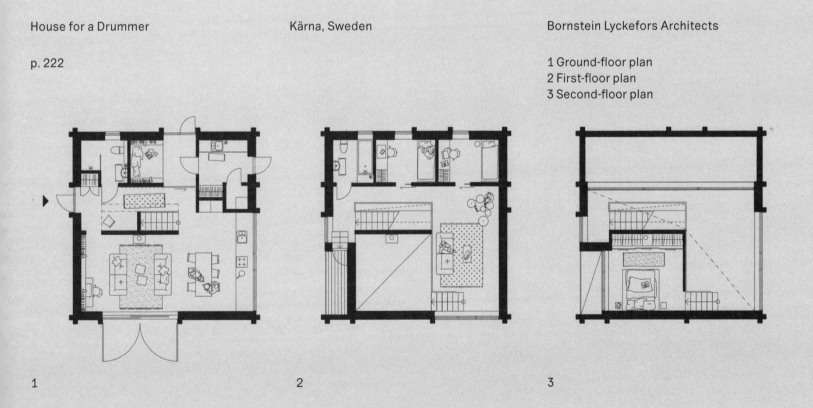

1

2

3

Plans

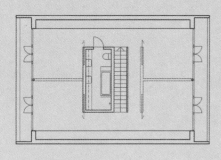

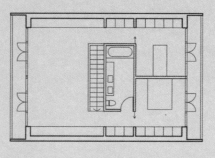

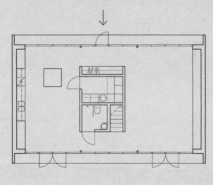

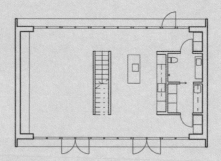

1

Villa G   Skanderborg, Denmark   C. F. Møller

p. 234   1 Plan

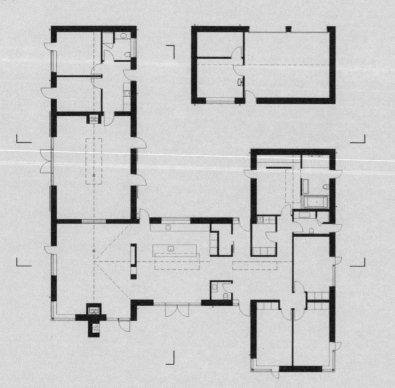

1

　　　　Borlänge, Sweden　　　　Murman Arkitekter

p. 240

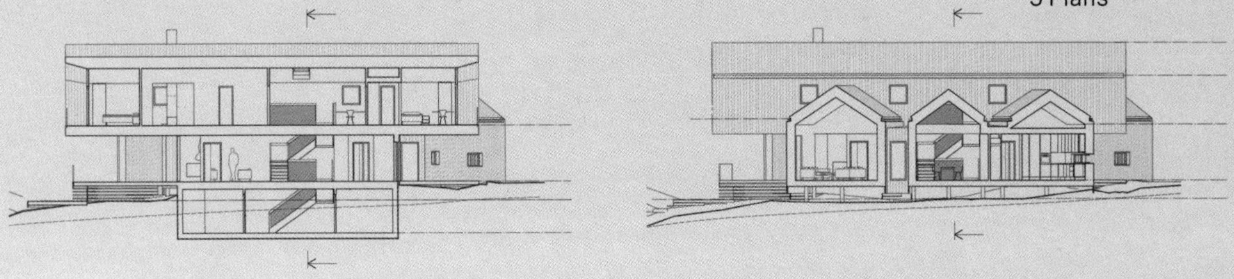

1

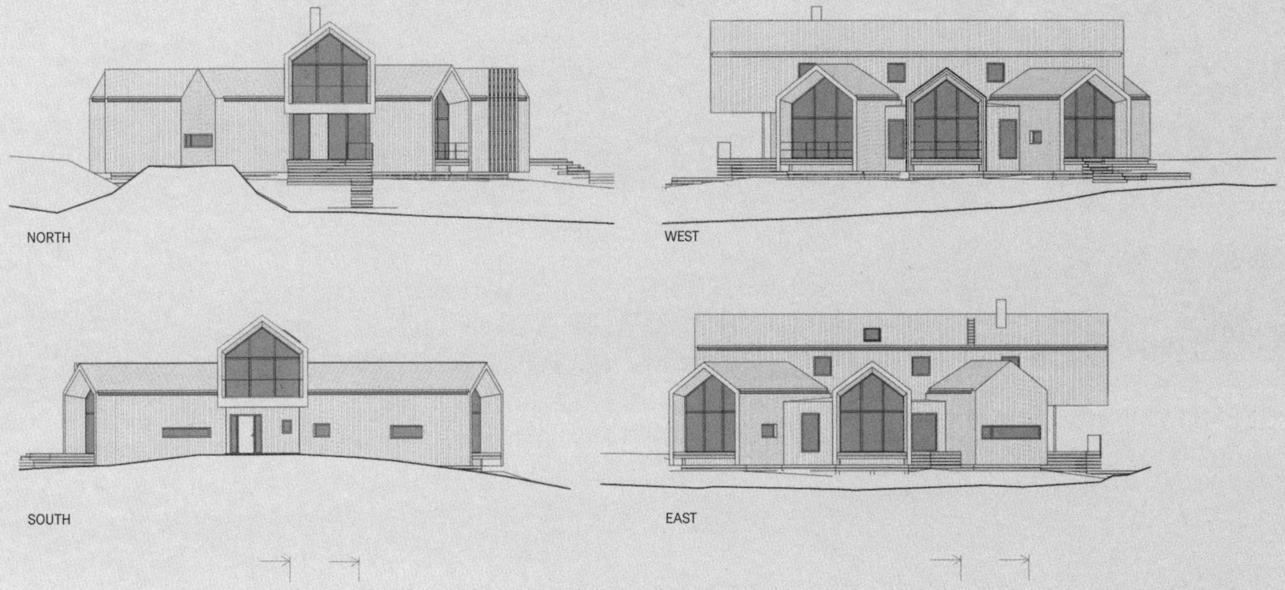

NORTH

WEST

SOUTH

EAST

2

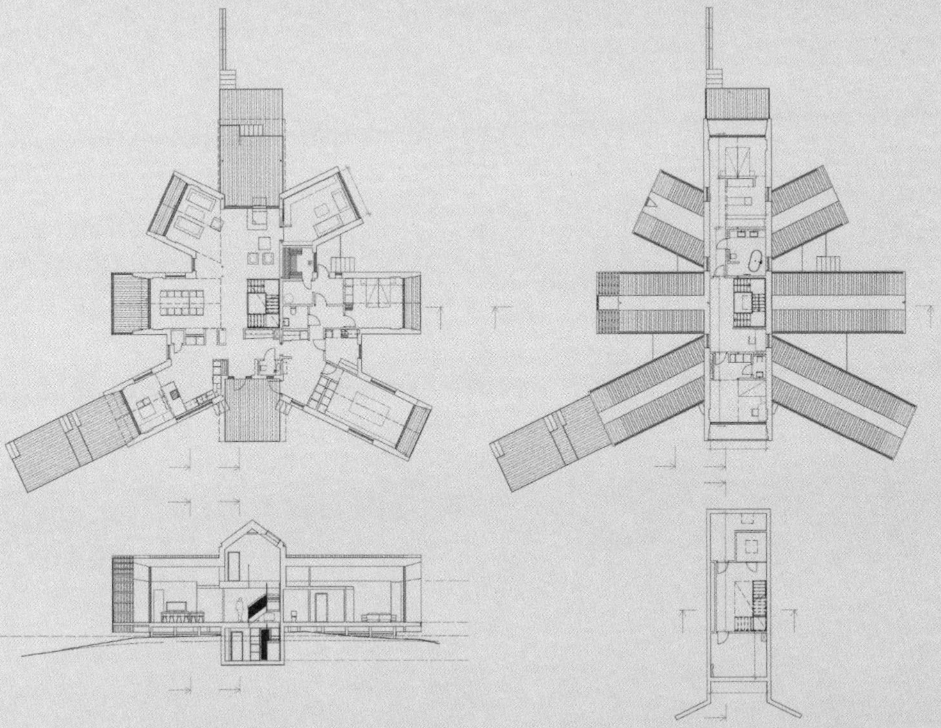

3

Plans

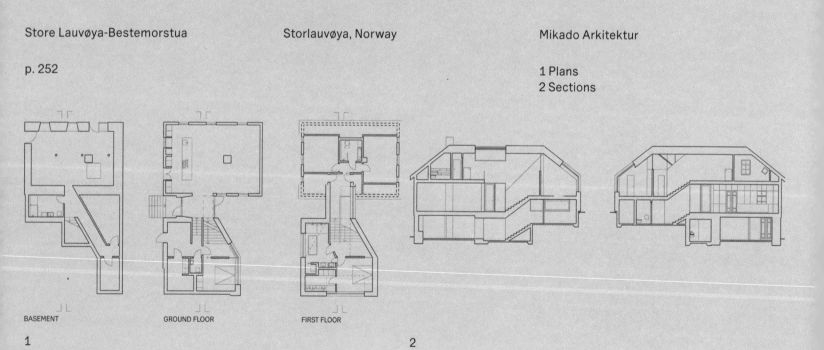

1

2

Store Lauvøya-Bestemorstua   Storlauvøya, Norway   Mikado Arkitektur

p. 252

1 Plans
2 Sections

BASEMENT   GROUND FLOOR   FIRST FLOOR

1   2

House Riihi

p. 256

Alajärvi, Finland

OOPEAA

1 Plans
2 Elevations

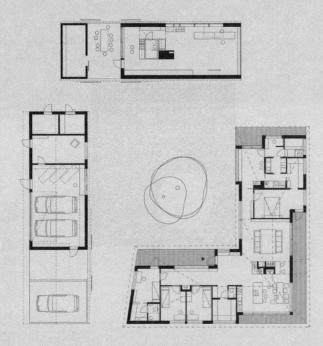

1

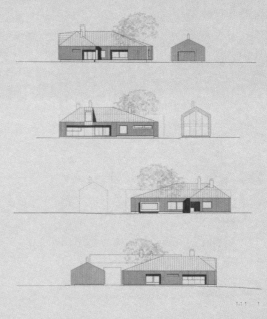

2

Villa Blåbär

p. 262

Nacka, Sweden

PS Arkitektur

1 Ground-floor plan
2 First-floor plan

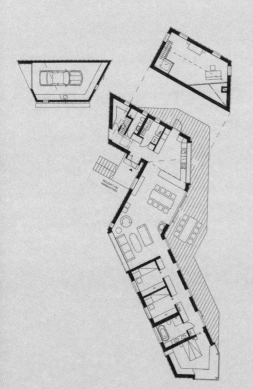

1

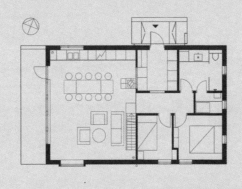

2

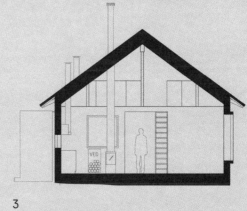

3

Plans

Villa N1

Frösakull, Sweden

Jonas Lindvall A & D

p. 268

1 Plan
2 Axonometric

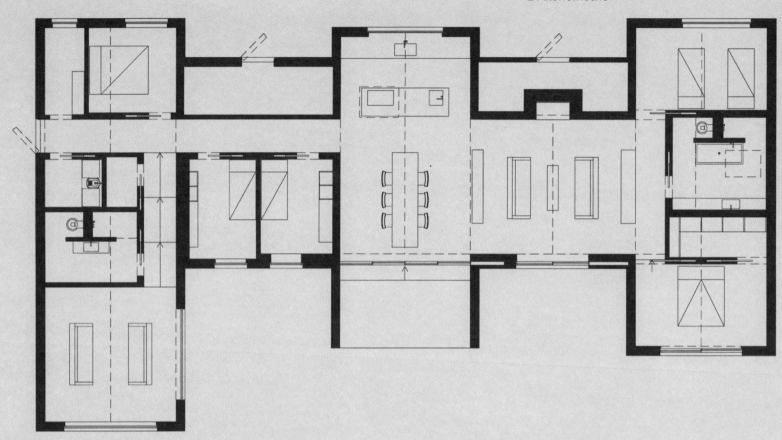

1

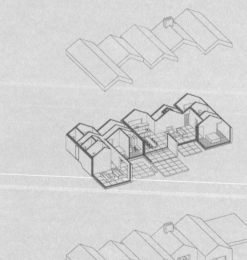

2

Split View Mountain Lodge

Geilo, Norway

Reiulf Ramstad Arkitekter

p. 274

1 Plans
2 Sections

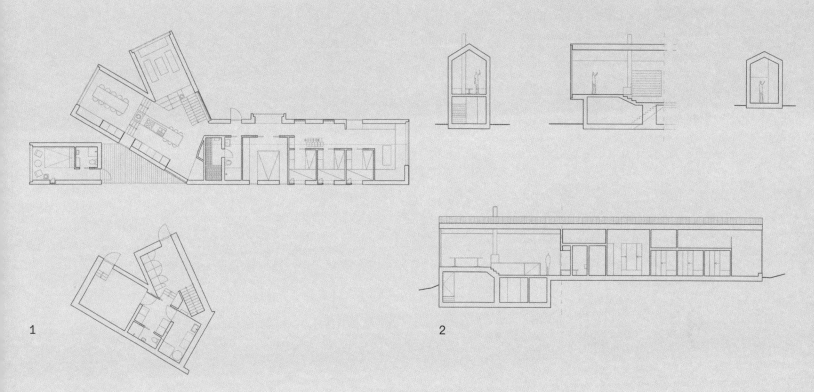

1

2

Villa Moelven

Stockholm, Sweden

Arkitektstudio Widjedal Racki

p. 282

1 Plan (levels 1 + 2)
2 Plan (levels 3, 4 + 5)
3 Plan (levels 6, 7 + 8)

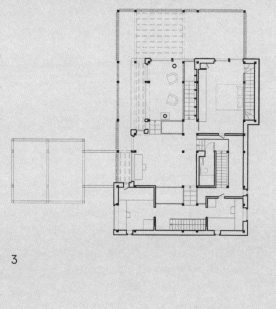

1

2

3

Project credits

Norderhov Cabin (p. 14)
Hønefoss, Norway
Architect: Atelier Oslo
Design team: Nils Ole Bae Brandtzæg,
Thomas Liu, Marius Mowe, Jonas Norsted,
Juan Ruiz, Bosheng Gan, Sveinn Thorarinsson,
Emmanuel Ferm
Consultants: Estatikk AS v/ Sivilingeniør Ole
Morten Braathen, Aps AS v/Kåre Wærnes,
Moelven Limtre AS v/ Rolf Evensen, Concept
Design v/Fredrik Eng
Main contractor: Byggmester Bård Bredesen
Area: 80 m² (860 sq ft)
Completed: 2014

Cabin Ustaoset (p. 20)
Ustaoset, Norway
Architect: Jon Danielsen Aarhus
Manufacturers: Kebony, Jatak, Norske
metallfasader
Contractor: TG-Bygg Geilo
Area: 72 m² (775 sq ft)
Completed: 2016

Gotland Summerhouse (p. 28)
Gotland, Sweden
Architects: Enflo Arkitekter, DEVE Architects
Lead architects: Jens Enflo, Morten Vedelsbøl
Engineer: Algeba Byggkonsulter
Builder: FideBygg & Snickeri
Area: 104 m² (1,120 sq ft)
Completed: 2012

Gudbrandslie Cabin (p. 34)
Tyinkrysset, Norway
Architect: Helen & Hard
Design team: Reinhard Kropf, Karen Jansen,
Moritz Groba, Nadine Engberding
Completed: 2015

Hytte Hvasser (p. 40)
Hvasser, Norway
Architect: Hille Strandskogen Architects

Villa Buresø (p. 46)
Slangerup, Denmark
Architect: Mette Lange Architects
Area: 238 m² (2,560 sq ft)
Completed: 2014

Österklint 20 (p. 52)
Bungenäs, Sweden
Architect: Skälsö Arkitekter
Completed: 2015

Bjellandsbu-Åkrafjorden Cabin (p. 60)
Etne, Norway
Architect: Snøhetta
Area: 35 m² (375 sq ft)
Completed: 2013

Arctic Treehouse Hotel (p. 66)
Rovaniemi, Finland
Architect: Studio Puisto
Lead architects: Willem van Bolderen,
Emma Johansson, Mikko Jakonen
Structural design: RV-rakenne Ky
Area: 1,450 m² (15,600 sq ft)
Completed: 2016

Archipelago House (p. 72)
Husarö, Sweden
Architect: Tham & Videgård
Lead architects: Bolle Tham, Martin Videgård
Area: 3,250 m² (34,980 sq ft)
Completed: 2006

Cabin Vindheim (p. 78)
Sjoga, Norway
Architect: Vardehaugen
Design team: Håkon Matre Aasarød, Berta
Gaztelu, Joana Branco, Kurt Breitenstein
Area: 65 m² (700 sq ft)
Completed: 2016

Åre Solbringen (p. 84)
Åre, Sweden
Architect: Waldemarson Berglund Arkitekter
Completed: 2010

Slävik Summerhouse (p. 92)
Lysekil, Sweden
Architect: Mats Fahlander
Area: 90 m² + 28 m² (970 sq ft + 300 sq ft)
Completed: 2011

Folded Roof House (p. 100)
Muskö, Sweden
Architect: Claesson Koivisto Rune
Completed: 2008

Aluminium Cabin (p. 108)
Nøtterøy, Norway
Architect: Jarmund/Vigsnæs Arkitekter
Lead architects: Einar Jarmund, Håkon
Vigsnæs, Alessandra Kosberg, Ane Sønderaal
Tolfsen
Area: 90 m² (970 sq ft)
Completed: 2013

Split House (p. 114)
Asker, Norway
Architect: Jarmund/Vigsnæs Arkitekter
Lead architects: Einar Jarmund, Håkon
Vigsnæs, Alessandra Kosberg, Stian
Schjelderup, Claes Cho Heske Ekornås
Area: 360 m² (3,875 sq ft)
Completed: 2013

Weekend House (p. 120)
Sildegarnsholmen, Norway
Architect: Knut Hjeltnes Sivilarkitekter
Completed: 2016

Vega Hytte (p. 124)
Vega, Norway
Architect: Kolman Boye Architects
Lead architects: Erik Kolman Janouch, Victor
Boye Julebæk
Area: 140 m² (1,507 sq ft)
Completed: 2012

Lille Arøya (p. 130)
Larvik, Norway
Architect: Lund Hagem Architects
Area: 75 m² (807 sq ft)
Completed: 2014

Stupet (p. 136)
Omberg, Sweden
Architect: Petra Gipp Arkitektur
Lead architects: Petra Gipp, Maria Videgård,
Erika Vegerfors
Area: 116 m² (1,250 sq ft)
Completed: 2013

Fleinvær Refugium (p. 142)
Fleinvær, Norway
Architects: TYIN Tegnestue, Rintala
Eggertsson
Manufacturers: Kebony, Norsk Spon, Livos
Naturmaling
Carpentry: Tømrer Stangvik, Andrew Devine,
Ruben Stranger
Engineer: Harboe Leganger
Welding: Hanmo
Area: 123 m² (1,325 sq ft)
Completed: 2017

Manshausen Island Resort (p. 150)
Steigen, Norway
Architect: Stinessen Arkitektur
Lead architect: Snorre Stinessen
Manufacturers: Sika
Completed: 2015

Summerhouse Lagnö (p. 156)
Stockholm, Sweden
Architect: Tham & Videgård
Design team: Martin Videgård, Bolle Tham,
Anna Jacobsson
Structural engineer: Sweco (Mathias
Karlsson)
Area: 140 m² (1,507 sq ft)
Completed: 2012

Villa Björnberget (p. 164)
Nacka, Sweden
Architect: Delin Arkitektkontor
Completed: 2017

Townhouse (p. 172)
Landskrona, Sweden
Architect: Elding Oscarson
Structural engineer: Konkret
Builder: Skånebygg
Area: 125 m² (1,346 sq ft)
Completed: 2009

Mölle by the Sea (p. 178)
Mölle, Sweden
Architect: Elding Oscarson
Manufacturers: panoramah!
Area: 300 m² (3,230 sq ft)
Completed: 2013

Villa Wienberg (p. 184)
Aarhus, Denmark
Architects: Wienberg Architects,
Friis & Moltke Architects
Engineer: Tri-Consult A/S
Area: 184 m² (1,980 sq ft)
Completed: 2008

Villa S (p. 190)
Bergen, Norway
Architect: Saunders Architecture
Lead architect: Todd Saunders
Completed: 2015

Roof House (p. 196)
Copenhagen, Denmark
Architect: Sigurd Larsen
Manufacturers: Velfac, Vitral
Area: 150 m² (1,615 sq ft)
Completed: 2016

Villa R (p. 202)
Ljungskile, Sweden
Architect: Arkitekterna Krook & Tjäder
Lead architect: Johan von Wachenfeldt
Design team: Maria Lundahl, Christian

Hammarström
Landscape architect: Cris Delisle
Area: 600 m² (6,460 sq ft)

Villa Kristina (p. 208)
Gothenburg, Sweden
Architect: Wingårdh Arkitektkontor
Area: 182 m² (883 sq ft)
Completed: 2014

Four Cornered Villa (p. 216)
Virrat, Finland
Architect: Avanto Architects
Structural design: Konstru Oy (Jorma Eskola)
Electrical design: Virtain Sähkötyö Oy (Väinö
Sipilä)
Budget: €150, 000
Area: 78 m² + 24 m² (840 sq ft + 258 sq ft)
Completed: 2010

House for a Drummer (p. 222)
Kärna, Sweden
Architect: Bornstein Lyckefors Architects
Lead architect: Andreas Lyckefors
Design team: Per Bornstein, Johan Olsson,
Caroline Jokiniemi, Viktor Stansvik, Monica
Warwick, Emil Lundin, Edvard Nyman
Area: 163 m² (1,755 sq ft)
Completed: 2016

Plus House (p. 228)
Vendelsö, Sweden
Architect: Claesson Koivisto Rune
Completed: 2007

Villa G (p. 234)
Skanderborg, Denmark
Architect: C. F. Møller
Construction: Brdr. Thybo
Area: 435 m² + 110 m² + 75 m²
(4,682 sq ft + 1,184 sq ft + 807 sq ft)
Completed: 2012

Villa Sunnanö (p. 240)
Borlänge, Sweden
Architect: Murman Arkitekter
Design team: Hans Murman, Truls Håkansson,
Per Sjöberg, Mattias Sköldborg, Anna
Wallerstedt Öberg, Helena Ljungberg, Tuva
Berg
Manufacturers: Dinesen, Velfac
Area: 322 m² (3,466 sq ft)
Completed: 2015

Slutterupgård (p. 246)
Hørsholm, Denmark
Architect: Henning Larsen

Store Lauvøya-Bestemorstua (p. 252)
Storlauvøya, Norway
Architect: Mikado Arkitektur
Manufacturer: Schüco
Collaborator: Poulsson/Pran Arkitekter
Civil engineer: Ottar Langehaug
Area: 300 m² (3,230 sq ft)
Completed: 2013

House Riihi (p. 256)
Alajärvi, Finland
Architect: OOPEAA
Lead architect: Anssi Lassila
Project architect: Jussi-Pekka Vesala
Design team: Iida Hedberg, Hanna-Kaarina
Heikkilä, Tommi Heinonen, Juha Pakkala
Area: 479 m² (5,156 sq ft)
Completed: 2014

Villa Blåbär (p. 262)
Nacka, Sweden
Architect: PS Arkitektur
Lead architect: Peter Sahlin
Project architect: Leif Johannsen
Assisting architects: Therese Svalling
(models), Beata Denton (lighting)
Contractor: Valento Bygg
Area: 170 m² (1,830 sq ft)
Completed: 2012

Villa N1 (p. 268)
Frösakull, Sweden
Architect: Jonas Lindvall A & D
Lead architect: Jonas Lindvall
Manufacturers: panoramah!, Architectural
Solutions, Wastberg, Rappgo, Stolab
Area: 190 m² (2,045 sq ft)
Completed: 2014

Split View Mountain Lodge (p. 274)
Geilo, Norway
Architect: Reiulf Ramstad Arkitekter
Area: 130 m² (1,400 sq ft)
Completed: 2013

Villa Moelven (p. 282)
Stockholm, Sweden
Architect: Arkitektstudio Widjedal Racki
Area: 220 m² (2,368 sq ft)
Completed: 2015

Project credits

Directory

Jon Danielsen Aarhus (p. 20)
Oslo, Norway
jdaa.no

Arkitekterna Krook & Tjäder (p. 202)
Gothenburg, Sweden
krooktjader.se

Arkitektstudio Widjedal Racki (p. 282)
Stockholm, Sweden
wrark.se

Atelier Oslo (p. 14)
Oslo, Norway
atelieroslo.no

Avanto Architects (p. 216)
Helsinki, Finland
avan.to

Bornstein Lyckefors Architects (p. 222)
Gothenburg, Sweden
bornsteinlyckefors.se

Claesson Koivisto Rune (pp. 100, 228)
Stockholm, Sweden
claessonkoivistorune.se

Delin Arkitektkontor (p. 164)
Stockholm, Sweden
delinarkitektkontor.se

DEVE Architects (p. 28)
Holte, Denmark
deve.dk

Elding Oscarson (pp. 172, 178)
Stockholm, Sweden
eldingoscarson.com

Enflo Arkitekter (p. 28)
Stockholm, Sweden
enflo.se

Mats Fahlander (p. 92)
Stockholm, Sweden
matsfahlander.com

Friis & Moltke Architects (p. 184)
Aarhus, Denmark
friis-moltke.dk

Petra Gipp Arkitektur (p. 136)
Stockholm, Sweden
gipparkitektur.se

Helen & Hard (p. 34)
Stavanger and Oslo, Norway
helenhard.no

Hille Strandskogen Architects (p. 40)
Oslo, Norway
hsark.no

Knut Hjeltnes Sivilarkitekter (p. 120)
Oslo, Norway
hjeltnes.as

Jarmund/Vigsnæs Arkitekter (pp. 108, 114)
Oslo, Norway
jva.no

Kolman Boye Architects (p. 124)
Stockholm, Sweden
kolmanboye.com

Mette Lange Architects (p. 46)
Copenhagen, Denmark
mettelange.com

Henning Larsen (p. 246)
Copenhagen, Denmark
henninglarsen.com

Sigurd Larsen (p. 196)
Berlin, Germany
sigurdlarsen.com

Jonas Lindvall A & D (p. 268)
Limhamn, Sweden
jonaslindvall.com

Lund Hagem Architects (p. 130)
Oslo, Norway
lundhagem.no

Mikado Arkitektur (p. 252)
Oslo, Norway
mikadoarkitektur.no

C. F. Møller (p. 234)
Aarhus, Denmark
cfmoller.com

Murman Arkitekter (p. 240)
Stockholm, Sweden
murman.se

OOPEAA (p. 256)
Seinäjoki, Finland
oopeaa.com

PS Arkitektur (p. 262)
Stockholm, Sweden
psarkitektur.se

Reiulf Ramstad Arkitekter (p. 274)
Oslo, Norway
reiulframstadarchitects.com

Rintala Eggertsson (p. 142)
Oslo, Norway
ri-eg.com

Saunders Architecture (p. 186)
Bergen, Norway
saunders.no

Skälsö Arkitekter (p. 52)
Visby, Sweden
skalso.se

Snøhetta (p. 58)
Oslo, Norway
snohetta.com

Stinessen Arkitektur (p. 150)
Tromsø, Norway
snorrestinessen.com

Studio Puisto (p. 66)
Helsinki, Finland
studiopuisto.fi

Tham & Videgård (pp. 72, 156)
Stockholm, Sweden
thamvidegard.se

TYIN Tegnestue (p. 142)
Trondheim, Norway
tyinarchitects.com

Vardehaugen (p. 78)
Oslo, Norway
vardehaugen.no

Waldemarson Berglund Arkitekter (p. 84)
Stockholm, Sweden
waldemarson.se

Wienberg Architects (p. 184)
Højbjerg, Denmark
wienbergarchitects.dk

Wingårdh Arkitektkontor (p. 208)
Gothenburg, Sweden
wingardhs.se

Photo credits

Dominic Bradbury is a journalist and writer specializing in architecture and design. He is the author of many books on the subject, including *Off the Grid*, *Mountain Modern*, *New Brazilian House*, *Vertical Living*, *Mid-Century Modern Design*, *The Iconic Interior*, *Waterside Modern*, and *The Iconic House*, all published by Thames & Hudson.

The author would like to express his sincere thanks to all of the architects, designers and homeowners featured in this book for their much valued assistance and support. Thanks also to Lucas Dietrich, Elain McAlpine, Fleur Jones, Evie Tarr and the rest of the team at Thames & Hudson, Ida Bentsen and Maria Rose at Heydays, and to the following: Faith Bradbury, Niall Harman, Carrie Kania, Richard Powers and Gordon Wise.

To Cecily

On the cover: Vega Hytte, Vega, Norway, by Kolman Boye Architects.
Photo: Åke E:son Lindman
On p. 1 Villa Kristina, Gothenburg, Sweden, by Wingårdh Arkitektkontor
On p. 3: Fleinvær Refugium, Fleinvær, Norway, by TYIN Tegnestue and Rintala Eggertsson

First published in the United Kingdom in 2019 by
Thames & Hudson Ltd, 181A High Holborn, London WC1V 7QX

First published in the United States of America in 2019 by
Thames & Hudson Inc., 500 Fifth Avenue, New York, New York 10110

Reprinted 2021

New Nordic Houses © 2019 Thames & Hudson Ltd, London
Text © 2019 Dominic Bradbury

Designed by Heydays

British Library Cataloguing-in-Publication Data
A catalogue record for this book is available from the British Library

Library of Congress Control Number 2019932281

ISBN 978-0-500-02155-2

Printed and bound in China by Toppan Leefung Printing Limited

Be the first to know about our new releases,
exclusive content and author events by visiting
thamesandhudson.com
thamesandhudsonusa.com
thamesandhudson.com.au